Cooking for Baby

Wholesome, homemade, delicious
foods for 6 to 18 months

Recipes by Lisa Barnes

Photographs by Tucker + Hossler

A Fireside Book
Published by Simon & Schuster
New York   London   Toronto   Sydney

contents

introducing solids

Beginning solid foods is one of the great milestones of the first year of life. It is one of those subjects that everyone has an opinion about, along with whether your child's feet are cold without socks or whether she ought to be crawling by now.

There's No Rush

Just a generation or two ago, babies were commonly started on solid food at the tender age of 6 weeks. The advice has changed, and most experts now recommend exclusive breast-feeding (or formula feeding) for the first several months. The feeding of solids should wait until baby is 6 months old. Foods may be offered a little sooner, at 4 months, but earlier introduction of food has been linked to allergies, diabetes, and obesity.

Parents often worry that baby needs more to eat than just milk or formula before the age of 6 months, and a baby going through a growth spurt can certainly seem ravenous. But babies can usually thrive for about this long on a liquid diet alone. In fact, breast milk or formula should make up the major part of a child's diet until her first birthday. Until then, rather than supplying baby's primary source of nutrition, feeding solids is a way for parents to let their baby explore a world of new tastes, textures, and temperatures, practice the skills of eating, and to learn to enjoy and appreciate the social aspects of mealtime.

Follow Baby's Cues

The best way to tell whether your baby is ready to start solids is to watch for cues. Here are some signals that show the time is right to begin offering food:

- Your baby is able to sit up well on her own, without your assistance.

- Your baby is able to turn her head away to refuse the food you are offering.

- Your baby develops a persistent pattern of remaining hungry after the usual feeding.

- Your baby stares at you when you eat or grabs for your food.

- Your baby can swallow pureed food, rather than reflexively spitting it out.

Ages & Stages
The recipes in this cookbook are divided into chapters by ages that correspond to general patterns of development. Keep in mind that every baby develops differently, and that you and your pediatrician are the best judges of what foods your baby should be eating, and when. If you have any special health concerns, such as allergies, discuss these issues with a health professional and be guided by his or her advice.

wholesome & homemade

Do you eat a lot of jarred, canned, or processed food? If the answer is no, then why should your baby? The foods you give your baby now, in the earliest months, will help shape your child's taste for many years to come.

Organic Living
To reduce your baby's exposure to toxins, choose organic ingredients for baby food whenever possible. It is especially important to purchase organic thin-skinned fruits and vegetables, such as apples or potatoes, since these absorb pesticides more readily than other produce. It is also wise to buy organic versions of fatty foods, such as meats, dairy, and oils. Pesticides and other environmental toxins tend to be stored in fat cells.

If you feed your baby only bland, processed jarred baby food and cereal, your baby will become accustomed to bland, processed food. On the other hand, if you feed your baby a variety of fresh fruits, vegetables, grains, and meats flavored with herbs and spices, you are priming his palate for a lifetime of healthful eating habits and culinary enjoyment. The benefits of making baby food at home are numerous:

● **It's unadulterated** You know exactly what goes into the food you make; there aren't any preservatives or fillers.

● **It's more versatile** Homemade puree can be diluted with breast milk, formula, or vegetable-cooking water for extra nutrition. As your baby grows, you can make his food just as thick and chunky as he can handle, helping his eating skills progress naturally.

● **It's more varied** Not every vegetable, fruit, grain, or meat is available in the form

of store-bought baby food. But you can cook and puree any food you and baby like.

● **It's more nutritious** Jarred baby food is heated to extremely high temperatures during processing, which destroys certain heat-sensitive vitamins more thoroughly than ordinary cooking does.

Of course, prepared baby food is a convenience and might play a role in any family pantry. But for parents who enjoy cooking and eating good meals, there is no reason not to include baby and start exposing him to the kinds of foods he will soon eat along with the rest of the family.

Making homemade baby food does require time and energy, both in short supply when you have a new infant. But by cooking in batches and freezing food (see page 15), you can make homemade baby food nearly as convenient as jarred.

introducing solids

start simple

At 6 months, your baby's digestive system is still new. The first foods you offer should be the most mild and digestible ones.

Introducing solids to your baby is a slow process of building a repertoire. With each new food you offer baby, you are shaping her taste and testing her tolerance. Some foods might not agree with her, causing a rash, gas, constipation, diarrhea, or vomiting. For this reason, new foods should be introduced one at a time. If a food doesn't agree with your baby, it might take a day or two for this to become apparent. So when you introduce a new food, feed it to your baby for at least 3 days before you introduce another new food. If your baby or family has allergic tendencies, you can extend this testing period to 5 or 7 days. This gradual approach to introducing new foods makes it easier to identify the culprit if there is any problem.

First Tastes

These foods are digestible and nutritious, and usually agree with babies:

- rice
- millet
- barley
- sweet potato & yam
- pumpkin & squash
- potato
- cooked apple
- cooked pear
- avocado
- banana

Gassy Foods

If your baby suffers from gassiness or colic, these foods might worsen the problem:

- beans
- peas
- lentils
- broccoli
- cabbage
- cauliflower
- cow's milk
- cucumber
- onion

Allergenic Foods

Many foods can be allergenic, but the majority of bad reactions are caused by a handful of foods:

- cow's milk
- egg white
- fish
- shellfish
- nuts
- peanuts
- soy
- strawberry
- wheat

preparing baby food

Cooking baby's food is manageable when you cook in batches. If you can reserve time on Sunday morning and Wednesday evening for meal preparation, you can have home-cooked foods for your baby all week long, even if you're away at work full-time.

Keep It Clean

When your baby is 6 months old, you no longer need to boil or sterilize his utensils, but you do still need to wash your hands and all cooking surfaces and utensils thoroughly with hot water and soap. Keep perishable foods cold and use separate containers and surfaces for raw meat and poultry. Wash all produce thoroughly, even if it's organic.

Or, if you cook in large batches and use the freezer, you can do the cooking less often.

Best Cooking Methods

Baby's first foods will likely be steamed or poached. These are simple cooking methods that don't require added fat, which may be hard for baby to digest at the beginning. Steaming is an especially good method to use because the food does not come in direct contact with water, which leaches away nutrients. Poaching is like simmering, but uses less water and keeps the heat low and gentle: big bubbles should rise slowly when you are poaching.

Roasting is another good cooking method for baby's food, especially for hardy root vegetables and meats. It's very simple to do, and if you set a timer you can go freely about your other tasks while you are preparing baby's dinner.

Whenever food you are cooking for baby, cook it until very tender, but don't overdo it. The longer you cook, the more nutrients you'll lose, and sometimes the flavor of a vegetable suffers when it is overdone.

Tools You'll Need

Using the right equipment helps simplify baby-food preparation. A steamer basket, a saucepan, a baking pan, and a food processor or blender are all you really need to make a wide range of foods for young babies. For pureeing, either a food processor or a blender will work, and you can also puree a food by cranking it through a food mill, by pushing it through a sieve with a wooden spoon or spatula, or by mashing it with a potato masher. Each method produces a different texture that is fun for baby to explore. Temperature-sensitive spoons help you make sure that baby's food is not too hot to eat.

storing baby food

If you're cooking homemade foods for your baby, you will soon become well acquainted with your freezer. Making baby food in batches, dividing it into serving-sized portions, and freezing it makes homemade baby food nearly as convenient as jarred.

Freezing Foods

As a general rule, freshly cooked food will keep for 3 days in the refrigerator or for 3 months in the freezer. When you've made up a batch of puree using a recipe from this book, set aside some for the refrigerator and freeze the rest. Let the food cool for about half an hour to room temperature before you put it in cold storage. Covered ice-cube trays are ideal for freezing baby serving–sized portions of puree. Just freeze them until hard, then transfer the frozen cubes to a freezer-weight plastic bag for storage. As baby grows and her portions get larger, small glass storage containers with lids can go from freezer to refrigerator to microwave—with none of the concern that comes with putting plastic containers in the microwave.

Be sure to label everything you freeze with the contents and the date. You may not recognize it a few weeks after storing it.

Thawing & Reheating

Both thawing and reheating can promote the growth of bacteria. Here are simple guidelines to keep foods as safe as possible for your baby:

● Thaw frozen foods in the refrigerator or in the microwave. Do not let baby's food sit out on a countertop for more than 1 hour, or 30 minutes in hot weather.

● To bring refrigerated purees to serving temperature, remove them from the refrigerator 15 to 30 minutes before serving.

● The best way to reheat purees is in a saucepan over medium-low heat. Microwave ovens are not recommended because they can cause hot spots in a bowl of food that would burn baby's mouth. Always check the temperature of baby's food carefully before feeding it to him.

● Do not freeze foods that have previously been frozen.

Half-Eaten Meals

When feeding your baby, be aware that the spoon will carry bacteria from her mouth to the bowl of food. A partially eaten bowl of food contains more bacteria than a freshly cooked batch, so saving this food and reheating it is usually unwise. It is better to dole out a small portion of food into a serving bowl before dipping baby's spoon into it. If you do reheat a partially eaten bowl of food, do so within a day or two.

first tastes

how to begin

What will baby's first food be? You'll hear and read plenty of differing advice, ranging from fortified baby rice cereal to mild, sweet fruits to nutritious vegetables and legumes. In fact, the order of introduction doesn't really matter.

First Foods to Try

These mild, nutritious foods are good choices for the youngest eaters.

Grains & Seeds
. . . .
rice cereal
barley cereal
millet cereal

Vegetables
. . . .
sweet potato or yam
butternut squash
  or pumpkin
potato

Fruits
. . . . .
apple (cooked)
avocado
banana
pear (cooked)

Legumes
. . . .
green peas

Some say that baby's first food should not be fruit, since fruits are high in natural sugars and this would give baby a sweet tooth. However, any baby who is breast-fed already has a preference for sweet foods, since breast milk is very sweet. For these babies, fruit may be a natural transition from a diet of mother's milk to solid foods.

Consistency Is Key

The first meals you give baby should have a very runny consistency—in other words, more liquid than solid. Young babies have a protective reflex that prevents them from swallowing thick solids, so swallowing food is a skill your baby needs to develop. You can use a food processor, a blender, a food mill, or an old-fashioned sieve and spoon to puree everything, thinning the texture by adding water, breast milk, or formula. (Later on, when you want to thicken a watery puree, try adding baby cereal.)

Easy Does It

Introduce new foods gradually, one at a time, and watch for adverse reactions. Each new food should be offered to baby for at least 3 days before you try the next one. Serve baby's first meals early in the day, so that if she does have an adverse reaction to a food within a few hours of eating it, the reaction is less likely to occur in the middle of the night when the household is asleep.

Keep It Light

Baby's mealtimes should always be pleasant and engaging. You might need to look up your sleeve for a few tricks: some babies need their parents to demonstrate how delicious their food is by eating a few bites themselves and raving about the flavor, or are more likely to open their mouths when "the airplane is flying into the hangar." Look to your baby's personality to guide you in sharing your pleasure in food.

how often & how much?

Keep in mind that for the first year, breast milk or formula should continue to be baby's primary source of nutrition. Offer a feeding of breast milk or formula before offering food, so that the food does not replace baby's usual feeding but merely supplements it.

When your baby is ready to begin solids, offer food just once a day for the first 2 weeks or month. The rest of her feedings will be the usual breast milk or formula. This may not seem like much, but her milk is full of fat and nutrition. As long as baby is growing well and the doctor is happy with her progress, she is getting enough to eat.

Follow Baby's Lead

Let your baby decide whether and how much he eats. A meal for a 6-month-old can range from a couple of teaspoons to a quarter cup. Offer the food on a spoon or fingertip. Losing interest, turning the head away, pursing the lips, swatting at the spoon, or spitting out food are signs that baby is done eating. It doesn't matter whether or not baby has finished all the food in his bowl. If your baby just doesn't seem interested in solid food in general, try again in a couple of days, or next week.

Babies Need Iron

The most common nutritional deficiency among babies is lack of iron, which causes anemia. Parents should be aware of this, as long-term untreated anemia in infancy can result in cognitive deficits, even years later. Full-term babies are born with a store of iron that lasts about 6 months; after this, they need to start getting iron through their food.

Some foods are naturally rich in iron, and others are supplemented with iron particularly for babies. For a 6-month-old (or younger), the best sources of iron are breast milk, iron-fortified formula, iron-fortified baby cereals, and prune puree or juice. Sometimes a pediatrician will recommend iron drops. Meat and poultry are great sources of iron, and small amounts of pureed meat can be introduced soon after baby begins solid food. For other iron-rich foods, see page 136.

A Drop of Water
Once your baby starts eating solid foods, start offering her water to drink as well. You can give it in a bottle or in a sippy cup—at 6 months, she is not too young to start learning to drink from a cup. This additional water helps baby digest his food and keeps him hydrated. At this age, you don't need to boil baby's water; she can drink tap water. If your family drinks bottled water, note that it is not generally fluoridated like tap water is. You can buy fluoridated bottled water for babies.

sweet pea puree

**peas, fresh or
frozen, 2 cups
(10 oz)**

MAKES 1½ CUPS

- Bring 1 inch water to a boil in a pot. Put peas in a steamer basket, set in pot, cover tightly, and steam until bright green and tender enough to mash easily with a fork, 5–7 minutes for fresh or hard frozen peas and 3 minutes for thawed frozen. Remove basket from pot, reserving cooking liquid. Rinse peas under running cold water to stop the cooking.

- Puree peas in a food processor until smooth. Add cooking liquid, breast milk, or formula to thin pea puree to a consistency that your baby can handle.

To store Refrigerate cooled pea puree in an airtight container for up to 3 days, or fill ice-cube trays or other containers to freeze for up to 3 months.

Homemade pea puree should be bright green, unlike the drab-colored jarred versions available at the supermarket. To help the peas retain their vibrant color, do not overcook them. Frozen peas are the next best thing to fresh spring peas: they're available year-round, and they will save you the time and effort of shelling.

baby's rice cereal

**brown rice,
¼ cup**

MAKES 1 CUP

Whole-grain brown rice retains the hull, which is removed to make white rice. The hull not only gives the rice its warm brown color, but also makes it more nutritious and flavorful than its white counterpart. As your baby grows and is able to handle thicker foods, turn to page 62 for a thicker version of this staple food.

- Put rice in a blender and pulverize into a powder, 3–5 minutes on medium to high speed.

- Bring 1 cup water to a simmer in a small saucepan over medium heat. Add brown rice powder and reduce heat to low. Cook, whisking constantly, until water is absorbed, 4–5 minutes.

- Add water, breast milk, or formula to thin the cereal to a consistency your baby can handle. As baby gets older and tries more foods, combine rice cereal with fruit or vegetable purees.

Notes Commercially prepared baby rice cereal is usually fortified with added iron. If you prepare rice cereal at home, discuss your baby's iron needs with your pediatrician. Young babies can get iron from a range of foods, including breast milk, formula, meat, poultry, prunes, and dried apricots. To store, refrigerate cooled cereal in an airtight container for up to 3 days, or fill ice-cube trays or other containers to freeze for up to 3 months.

6 months

zucchini puree

zucchini or other summer squash, 2 large or 3 small

MAKES 1½–2 CUPS

● Cut zucchini into rounds 1 inch thick. Bring 1 inch water to a boil in a pot. Put squash in a steamer basket, set in pot, cover tightly, and steam until very tender, 5–9 minutes, depending on size.

● Puree squash in a food processor until smooth. Additional liquid will not be needed. As baby gets older, add baby's cereal to thicken this liquidy puree, if desired.

Notes Since baby will eat the peel, be sure to buy organic squash if possible. To store, refrigerate cooled puree in an airtight container for up to 3 days, or fill ice-cube trays or other containers to freeze for up to 3 months.

Zucchini and other summer squashes, such as pattypan and crookneck, have watery flesh, tender seeds, and thin, edible skins. Zucchini is a good choice for baby's first green vegetable, because it is mild and digestible and delivers a wide assortment of nutrients, especially vitamin A, potassium, and magnesium.

winter squash puree

**butternut squash
or baking
pumpkin, 1¼ lb**

MAKES 2½ CUPS

Winter squashes
have hard, thick
skins and inedible
seeds. Butternut
squash, acorn
squash, and
pumpkin are the
most popular types,
but you can cook
any winter squash
this way. Roasting
brings out their
natural sugars
and rich flavor. Like
summer squashes,
winter squashes
offer a wide array of
vitamins, minerals,
and fiber, but they
are especially high
in vitamins A and C.

● Preheat oven to 350°F. With a heavy, sharp knife, cut squash in half. Scrape out seeds and fibrous strings and discard.

● Put squash, cut side down, in a baking pan. Pour water into pan to come ¼ inch up the sides of the squash. Roast until tender when pierced with a fork, 45 minutes–1 hour, depending on size. Let cool.

● Scoop out flesh and puree in a food processor until smooth. Add water, breast milk, or formula to thin squash to a consistency your baby can handle.

To store Refrigerate cooled puree in an airtight container for up to 3 days, or fill ice-cube trays or other containers to freeze for up to 3 months.

sweet potato puree

Sweet potatoes are nutritional powerhouses, packed with beta-carotene, fiber, vitamins A and C, and minerals such as iron and copper. Make them a staple food in your baby's diet. You will find different varieties with varying shades of flesh, from tan to yellow to deep orange (often labeled "yams").

sweet potatoes, 2, scrubbed

MAKES 2 CUPS

● Preheat oven to 425°F. Prick sweet potatoes with a small knife and place on a baking sheet.

● Roast until wrinkled and tender when pierced with the tip of a knife, 45–60 minutes. Let cool.

● Halve sweet potatoes, scoop out flesh from skins, and puree flesh in a food processor until smooth. Add water, breast milk, or formula to thin sweet potatoes to a consistency your baby can handle. As baby gets older and can eat thicker purees, mash some or all of the sweet potato with a fork.

Notes The cooking method above can also be used for baking potatoes. To store, refrigerate cooled puree in an airtight container for up to 3 days, or fill ice-cube trays or other containers to freeze for up to 3 months.

pear puree

ripe pears, 4, quartered and cored just before cooking

MAKES 2 CUPS

- Bring 1 inch water to a boil in a pot. Put pears in a steamer basket, set in pot, cover tightly, and steam until tender when pierced with the tip of a knife, 7–10 minutes, depending on ripeness

- Let cool and scrape flesh from skins. Puree pears in a food processor until smooth. As baby gets older, add baby's cereal to thicken this liquidy puree, if desired.

Notes Let pears ripen on a countertop. To store, refrigerate cooled puree in an airtight container for up to 3 days, or fill ice-cube trays or other containers to freeze for up to 3 months. Expect some slight discoloration during storing.

apple puree

Golden or Red Delicious apples, 6, quartered and cored just before cooking

MAKES 2 CUPS

- Bring 1 inch water to a boil in a pot. Put apples in a steamer basket, set in pot, cover tightly, and steam until tender when pierced with the tip of a knife, 10–12 minutes.

- Let cool, reserving cooking liquid. Scrape flesh from skins and puree in a food processor until smooth. Add reserved cooking liquid to thin puree, if desired.

Notes Refrigerate cooled apple puree in an airtight container for up to 3 days, or fill ice-cube trays or other containers to freeze for up to 3 months. Expect some slight discoloration during storing.

Pears and apples are both pleasing first foods for babies. Cooking them with the skin on retains more nutrients. Pears are high in fiber and can help with constipation, while apples can be binding. Golden and Red Delicious and Fujis have the least amount of acid, making them the best choices for young babies.

new flavors

exploring flavor

Many babies happily take to eating solid foods, while others are slow to warm to them. Let baby explore new flavors and textures at his own pace, with gentle encouragement from you. The more flavors he tries now, the more accepting of variety he will be later.

At first, baby's pureed foods should remain quite runny, but week by week you can gradually make them thicker, as baby shows he can handle them. Experiment with a sieve, food mill, potato masher, and a fork to create different consistencies. You can try mixing smooth purees with chunkier mashes, or thickening a thin puree with baby's cereal. By 8 months, some babies will start to pick up and chew soft finger foods. Even before they have very many teeth, babies can mash and gum their food well.

How Often & How Much?

Each month, start offering baby an additional daily meal, so that by 8 months he is eating 3 times a day. Continue to let baby eat as much solid food as he likes at each meal, preferably a short while after he has finished a feeding of breast milk or formula. This way, the breast milk or formula remains baby's main source of nutrition, and baby will not be overhungry and cranky at the beginning of a meal.

Keep introducing new foods one at a time, so that if one of them definitely doesn't agree with your child, you'll be able to identify which one it is. If your baby rejects a food or doesn't like the flavor, don't force or coax him to eat it—but don't give up, either. Offer it again on another day. It's common for babies to accept a food only after it becomes familiar, and it may take as many as 10 to 15 tries before this happens.

Once your baby has tried a few different foods, you can start mixing them together to create new combinations. In this chapter, recipes for single-food purees are followed by recipes for combinations of foods that your baby can try after he has had each of the ingredients on its own. Once you get into the swing of making baby's meals, try some new ingredient combinations of your own!

pure & simple

Some parents can't wait for baby to sample everything from their own adult dinner plates. If you do wish to feed baby pureed table foods, in addition to his own specially prepared foods, here are a few pointers. (See page 136 for more details on nutrition.)

Salt

Pureed table foods can be high in sodium from salt. Don't add salt to your baby's diet quite yet. Breast milk, formula, and many foods contain sodium naturally. Too much sodium can overload baby's system.

Sugar

Babies may have sweet tooths, but it's best to let them try each new food in its natural state and to learn to enjoy a variety of flavors. If you think a food, such as cereal or meat, needs sweetening, try adding a fruit puree. White sugar lacks nutrition, and babies should not eat honey until the age of 1; even cooked honey may contain potentially harmful botulism spores. Hold off on offering juice as well, even if diluted. Juice is high in sugar and lacks the fiber and many nutrients found in whole fruits and vegetables. It's a good idea for baby to develop a taste for plain water.

Fat

We adults are always hearing advice to cut the fat from our diets. Babies, however, need a high-fat diet. Breast milk, nature's perfect food for infants, is 40 to 50 percent fat, and high in cholesterol as well. Babies benefit not only from the "good" fats, such as those found in avocados and olive oil, but also from the saturated fats in such animal sources as meat and butter, which should be limited in the diet later in life. The fats to avoid giving your baby are trans fats, often labeled as "hydrogenated," found in processed and fast foods.

A Word on Milk

When they are ready for it, whole milk is a great nutrition source for toddlers. But stick to breast milk and formula until your baby is 1 year old. Cow's milk is the most common allergen among babies, is hard to digest, and interferes with iron absorption.

New Foods to Try

These nutritious foods are good choices for the 7- to 8-month set.

Fruits

apricot (cooked)
blueberry (cooked)
cherry (cooked)
cranberry (cooked)
peach & nectarine (cooked)
plum & prune (cooked)

Legumes

carob
green bean
lentils
split peas

Meat

lamb
turkey

asparagus puree

**asparagus,
1 bunch (about
1 lb), woody ends
snapped off**

MAKES ¾–1 CUP

- Bring 1 inch water to a boil in a pot. Put asparagus in a steamer basket, set in pot, cover tightly, and steam until tender and bright green, 7–9 minutes. Rinse asparagus under running cold water to stop the cooking.

- Puree asparagus in a food processor until smooth. Additional liquid will not be needed.

Notes Try this puree alone first, but if baby is reluctant to eat it, stirring in some apple or pear puree may tempt him. To store, refrigerate cooled puree in an airtight container for up to 3 days, or fill ice-cube trays or other containers to freeze for up to 3 months.

green beans with mint

**green beans,
½ lb, trimmed**

**fresh mint,
1 Tbsp chopped**

**olive oil, 2 Tbsp
(optional)**

MAKES ¾–1 CUP

- In a large frying pan over medium-high heat, bring 1 inch water to a boil. Add beans and return to a boil. Cover and cook until very tender and bright green, 7–9 minutes. Drain beans and rinse under running cold water to stop the cooking.

- Puree green beans with 2 Tbsp water and mint in a food processor until smooth. Stir in olive oil, if using, and serve.

Notes As baby gets older, you can offer green beans as finger food, first cut up and later whole. To store, refrigerate cooled puree in an airtight container for up to 3 days.

You may have more success getting your baby to eat green vegetables in the early months than a few years later, especially if you swirl in some fruit puree as shown opposite. Asparagus offers a wide range of vitamins: A, C, K, and several of the B vitamins. Green beans provide vitamin C and manganese, plus plenty of fiber.

baby's millet cereal

millet, ¼ cup

MAKES ½ CUP

- Put millet in a blender and pulverize into a powder, 1–2 minutes on medium to high speed.

- Bring 1 cup water to a simmer in a small saucepan over medium heat. Add millet powder and reduce heat to low. Cook, whisking constantly, until water is absorbed, 5–7 minutes.

- Add water, breast milk, or formula to thin cereal to a consistency your baby can handle. As baby gets older and tries more foods, combine millet cereal with fruit or vegetable purees.

To store Refrigerate millet in an airtight container for up to 3 days, or freeze in ice-cube trays or other containers for up to 3 months.

Two mild, easily digested grains, millet and barley are found in the dry bulk section of specialty- and natural-food stores. Both are excellent grains to include in your baby's diet, providing fiber and minerals such as phosphorus, manganese, and magnesium.

baby's barley cereal

pearl barley, ¼ cup

MAKES 1 CUP

- Put barley in a blender and pulverize into a powder, 5 minutes on medium to high speed.

- Bring 1 cup water to a simmer in a small saucepan over medium heat. Add barley powder and reduce heat to low. Cook, whisking constantly, until water is absorbed, 4–5 minutes.

- Add water, breast milk, or formula to thin cereal to a consistency your baby can handle. As baby gets older and tries more foods, combine barley cereal with fruit or vegetable purees.

To store Refrigerate barley in an airtight container for up to 3 days, or freeze in ice-cube trays or other containers for up to 3 months.

baby's lamb

vegetable oil for greasing

boneless lamb steak or chop, 1, 1 inch thick

MAKES ABOUT
¾ CUP

- Preheat oven to 400°F. Place lamb on a greased rack set in an aluminum foil–lined roasting pan. Roast, turning once, until cooked through and no longer pink, 12–14 minutes per side. Let cool.

- Coarsely chop lamb, then puree in a food processor for 1 minute. With machine running, add ¼ cup water. The texture will be pastelike. Add more liquid to thin lamb puree to a consistency that your baby can handle.

Notes When buying lamb, look for pink to light red meat with little fat, and trim off the excess. To store, refrigerate lamb puree in an airtight container for 1–2 days, or freeze for up to 1 month.

baby's turkey

ground turkey, ½ lb

MAKES ABOUT
1 CUP

- In a nonstick frying pan over medium heat, combine turkey and ¼ cup water. Cook, breaking up the turkey and stirring constantly, until meat is cooked through and no longer pink, 3–5 minutes. Let cool. Drain and reserve cooking liquid.

- Transfer turkey to a food processor and puree for 1 minute. With machine running, add reserved cooking liquid by the tablespoon. The texture will be pastelike. Add more liquid to thin puree to a consistency your baby can handle.

To store Refrigerate turkey puree in an airtight container for 1–2 days, or freeze for up to 1 month.

Red meat and poultry are good sources of iron and protein for a growing baby, and lamb and turkey are the best ones to start with because they're easy to digest. Meat purees are most palatable when blended with a fruit puree baby has already tried. Lamb has an assertive flavor that pairs well with prune (page 39) or dried apricot (page 39). To sweeten and smooth baby's turkey, stir in pureed apples (page 27) or pears (page 27).

whipped cauliflower

**cauliflower
or broccoli,
1 large head**

**unsalted butter,
2 Tbsp**

MAKES 2½ CUPS

Cauliflower puree, packed with vitamins and fiber, is a wonderful dinnertime alternative to plain mashed white potatoes. However, if your baby suffers from gassiness, stick with the potatoes for now. To serve the whole family, after dishing up baby's portion, stir in a dash of garlic salt and enjoy with grilled meats.

● Trim cauliflower and cut into similar-sized florets. Put florets in a pot with cold water to cover. Put lid on pot, bring to a boil over medium-high heat, and boil just until cauliflower is tender, 15–18 minutes. Be careful not to overcook, or cauliflower will separate and fall apart. Drain.

● While still hot, puree cauliflower with butter in a food processor until very smooth and creamy.

To store Refrigerate cooled cauliflower puree in an airtight container for up to 3 days, or fill ice-cube trays or larger containers to freeze for up to 3 months.

blueberry sauce

**blueberries, fresh
or thawed frozen,
2 cups or one
16-oz bag**

MAKES ¾ CUP

Sweet and delicious blueberries are one of nature's super-foods, loaded with disease-fighting antioxidants and vitamins. Dark red cherries have a similar nutritional profile. Neither is related to more allergenic berries such as raspberries and strawberries, so they can be introduced earlier into baby's diet.

● Puree blueberries in a food processor until smooth. There will be small pieces of peel in the puree. To remove them, put puree in a fine-mesh sieve over a small mixing bowl and push puree through sieve with a rubber spatula. The sauce will have a yogurtlike consistency.

● Heat puree in a small saucepan over medium-low heat until hot, 3–5 minutes. Let cool completely before serving.

Notes Heating this sauce after straining breaks down fibers and aids in digestion. Once your baby has tried blueberries, you may eliminate the step of heating the sauce—just blend and serve. To store, refrigerate cooled sauce in an airtight container for up to 3 days, or fill ice-cube trays or other containers to freeze for up to 3 months.

cherry puree

**sweet cherries,
fresh or thawed
frozen, 2 cups or
one 16-oz bag**

MAKES ¾ CUP

● Puree cherries in a food processor until smooth, stopping once or twice to scrape down the sides of the workbowl.

● Heat puree in a small saucepan over medium-low heat until hot, 3–5 minutes. Let cool completely before serving.

To store Refrigerate cooled puree in an airtight container for up to 3 days, or fill ice-cube trays or other containers to freeze for up to 3 months.

7 to 8 months

prune puree

pitted prunes, 8

MAKES 2 CUPS

- In a small saucepan over medium-high heat, combine prunes and 1½ cups water and bring to a boil. Reduce heat to low and simmer until tender, 8–10 minutes. Prunes should pierce easily with a fork. Remove from heat and let cool, reserving cooking liquid.

- Puree prunes in a food processor until smooth. Add cooking liquid to thin the puree to a consistency your baby can handle.

Notes You can dilute the remaining cooking liquid and give to baby to drink. To store, refrigerate cooled puree in an airtight container for up to 3 days, or fill ice-cube trays or other containers to freeze for up to 3 months. Prune cooking liquid or "juice" also freezes well.

dried-apricot puree

dried apricots, 1 cup

MAKES 1½ CUPS

- In a small saucepan over medium-high heat, combine apricots and 1 cup water and bring to a boil. Reduce heat to low and simmer until tender, about 10 minutes. Apricots should pierce easily with a fork. Remove from heat and let cool, reserving cooking liquid.

- Puree apricots in a food processor until smooth. Add cooking liquid to thin the puree to a consistency your baby can handle.

To store To store, refrigerate cooled puree or cooking liquid in an airtight container for up to 3 days, or fill ice-cube trays or other containers to freeze for up to 3 months.

Dried plums and apricots have great virtues as baby food. They are rich in iron and also contain vitamin C, which helps the body absorb iron. And, they are high in fiber. If your baby is suffering from constipation, these purees may well solve the problem. Feed just a small amount, as a little goes a long way. Choose dried fruits that are naturally sun-dried and not treated with sulfur dioxide or paraffin.

peach puree

**ripe peaches
or nectarines,
4, halved,
pitted, and cut
into even-sized
chunks**

MAKES 2 CUPS

● Bring 1 inch water to a boil in a pot. Put peaches in a steamer basket, set in pot, cover tightly, and steam until soft but not falling apart, 2–4 minutes, depending on ripeness. Peaches should pierce easily with a fork. Let cool.

● Scrape flesh from skins with a spoon, and puree in a food processor until smooth. Additional liquid will not be needed.

Notes Once baby has tried them cooked, ripe peaches may also be peeled and pureed without cooking. To store, refrigerate cooled puree in an airtight container for up to 3 days, or fill ice-cube trays or other containers to freeze for up to 3 months.

plum puree

**black plums,
6 medium,
halved and pitted**

MAKES 2 CUPS

● Bring 1 inch water to a boil in a pot. Put plums in a steamer basket, set in pot, cover tightly, and steam until soft but not falling apart, 2–3 minutes, depending on ripeness. Plums should pierce easily with a fork. Let cool.

● Scrape flesh from skins with a spoon, and puree in a food processor until smooth. Additional liquid will not be needed.

To store Refrigerate cooled puree in an airtight container for up to 3 days, or fill ice-cube trays or other containers to freeze for up to 3 months.

Peaches and plums   both members of the drupe family of fruits—are perfect summertime introductions. They make good purees for blending with other less-sweet foods, such as cereals, meats, and beans. If peaches are out of season, substitute frozen ones. Commercially frozen fruits and vegetables are picked when ripe and retain most of their nutrients, and organic ones are widely available.

herbs for baby

Some parents are reluctant to introduce herbs and spices to babies since typical jarred baby food is very bland. However, babies in many cultures are introduced to seasonings and flavorful foods early on. Let your own diet, your culture, and your baby be your guide. Treat herbs and spices like any other ingredient, introducing them one at a time, starting with milder ones when baby begins solid food and moving on into toddlerhood with the more pungent ones. If allergies run in the family, exercise caution when you introduce caraway, cinnamon, coriander, fennel, paprika, and saffron, which can cause reactions.

Basil	Minty, clovelike aroma. Pairs well with tomatoes, pasta, white beans, and asparagus.
Chives	Mild onion flavor. Best when sprinkled on potato, egg, and fish dishes.
Cilantro	Also known as fresh coriander. Adds an aromatic flavor to chicken, avocados, black beans, rice, corn, cucumbers, and carrots.
Dill	A delicate, fresh flavor. Pairs well with baked fish, peas, and artichokes.
Mint	Sharply aromatic flavor matches well with peas, green beans, eggplants, and lamb.
Oregano	A robust and pungent flavor. Pairs well with turkey, pastas, summer squashes, and tomatoes.
Parsley	Lends a mild, fresh taste to many dishes. The flat-leaf, or Italian, variety has more flavor and is easier to chop and chew than the curly type. Add to stock, carrots, and potatoes.
Rosemary	Bold piney and minty flavor. Best with beef, lamb, and grilled vegetables.
Sage	Yields a bitter, slightly musty and minty flavor. Complements pork, turkey, white beans, and summer squashes.
Tarragon	A subtle, aromatic licorice flavor. Pairs well with chicken, white fish, lamb, rice, and asparagus.
Thyme	Both mint and lemon tones. Add to roasted meats and poultry, fish, shellfish, beets, and potatoes.

spice it up

Spices and dried herbs are convenient to keep in the pantry. Warming whole or ground spices in a dry frying pan for a few seconds will bring out their flavors. Since they have lost their moisture, dried herbs are more concentrated in flavor than fresh ones. To substitute fresh herbs for dried, triple the amount. Before adding a fresh or dried herb to a dish, bruise or crush it with your fingers to release its flavor.

Allspice   Earthy, warm flavor. Pairs well with sweet potatoes, apples, pumpkins, and meat stews.

Cardamom   Spicy, sweet flavor with peppery tones. Pairs well with winter squash and curry dishes.

Cinnamon   Strong, spicy, sweet flavor. Lends depth to ricotta, butternut squashes, and oatmeal.

Cumin   Pungent spicy flavor. Add to potatoes, chicken, couscous, and curries.

Curry   Fragrant, mild to hot blend of spices. Works well with chicken, carrots, parsnips, and rice. Start with a mild blend for baby.

Fennel   Mild licorice flavor. Goes well with pork, cabbage, and poached fish.

Garlic   Pungent, hot flavor that mellows when cooked. Used as a seasoning when dried and ground, or as a seasoning, condiment, and ingredient in fresh form. Adds savory flavor to all meats and vegetables.

Ginger   Sweet-hot flavor. Pairs well with meats, pumpkin, carrots, and sweet potatoes.

Nutmeg   Slightly sweet and spicy flavor and aroma. Adds spice to ricotta cheese, spinach, pears, and rice pudding.

Paprika   Slightly sweet and bitter. Pairs well with baked fish, eggs, corn, and roasted potatoes.

Pepper   Both pungent black and milder white pepper go well with savory dishes. Add to meat, poultry, eggs, and vegetables.

Turmeric   Earthy and peppery flavor. Adds flavor and a bright yellow-orange color to potatoes, lentils, meat, and curry dishes.

Vanilla   Seeds and liquid extract are used to flavor baked goods, waffles, and pancakes.

baby's stock

asparagus spears, 6

leek, 1 large, cut into chunks (1 cup)

sweet potato, ½, peeled and cut into chunks (1 cup)

MAKES ABOUT 2 CUPS

This recipe is basic yet versatile. As the vegetables simmer, they release their nutrients into the cooking water. Once you have introduced 2 of the 3 vegetable ingredients to your baby, put the nutritious stock in his bottle in place of water, or use it as a liquid for poaching fish (page 58) and as an ingredient in other recipes.

● Put 1 qt (4 cups) cold water in a medium pot. Add asparagus, leek, and sweet potato and bring to a boil over high heat. Reduce heat to maintain a gentle simmer, and cover pot. Simmer until vegetables are very soft and cooking liquid is lightly flavored and colored, about 1 hour.

● Strain the broth through a sieve, reserving vegetables. The vegetables can be pureed or mashed for baby. Serve stock lukewarm or cooled in a cup or bottle, or use in other recipes.

Notes If you buy organic sweet potatoes, you can scrub them well but leave the peels on. To store, refrigerate stock in an airtight container for up to 3 days, or fill ice-cube trays or other containers to freeze for up to 3 months. If you're short on time and prefer to use store-bought broth, look for broth with no or reduced sodium and all-natural, recognizable ingredients that you have already introduced to your baby. Good-quality prepared broths in aseptic cartons are widely available, and some markets carry broths in the refrigerated or frozen section.

asparagus "risotto"

Arborio rice,
1/2 cup

Baby's Stock
(opposite) or
water, 1 cup

extra-virgin olive
oil or unsalted
butter, 1 tsp

fresh tarragon,
2 tsp minced

Asparagus Puree
(page 33),
1/3–2/3 cup

MAKES 1¾ CUPS

● Put rice, stock, and oil in a heavy-bottomed saucepan over medium-high heat and bring to a boil. Reduce heat to low and cook, stirring once, until liquid has been absorbed and rice is thick and creamy, about 15 minutes. Remove saucepan from heat, stir in tarragon, and let stand, covered, for 10 minutes. Fluff rice with fork, stir in asparagus puree, and check temperature before serving.

● If needed, puree the "risotto" with a food mill or in a food processor to a consistency your baby can handle.

Notes Butter, like yogurt and cheese, can be introduced to baby before age 1 because it is less likely to be allergenic than plain milk. To store, refrigerate cooled rice in an airtight container for up to 3 days, or fill ice-cube trays or larger containers to freeze for up to 3 months.

Traditionally, medium-grained rice such as Arborio is used in making risotto. This dish does not demand all of the stirring and attention that true risotto requires, but the rice still becomes a little creamy after cooking. If your baby is uncertain about eating asparagus or another green vegetable, she might find it more appealing as part of this comfort dish.

potato & butternut squash stew

butternut squash,
½ small, peeled
and seeded

yellow potatoes,
6 small, peeled

Fuji apple,
1 medium, peeled,
halved, and cored

extra-virgin olive
oil, 1 Tbsp

Baby's Stock
(page 44) or
water, 1½ cups

MAKES 4 CUPS

After baby tries potatoes, squash, and apple as single-food purees and is ready to move on to combinations, this is a great dish to introduce. You can adjust the texture according to your baby's stage: mash with a fork to make the stew thicker, or put some or all of it in the food processor for a smoother texture.

- Cut squash, potatoes, and apple into 1-inch chunks. You should have about 1 cup of each.

- Heat oil in a saucepan over medium-high heat. Add squash, potatoes, and apple and cook, stirring occasionally, 8–10 minutes. Apples will begin to turn golden. Add stock and bring to a boil. Reduce heat to maintain a gentle simmer, cover, and simmer until vegetables are soft, 30–35 minutes.

- Mash and combine with a wooden spoon, potato masher, or food processor to a consistency your baby can handle.

Notes For added convenience, look for cubed butternut squash in the freezer section of your supermarket. To store, refrigerate cooled stew in an airtight container for up to 3 days, or fill ice-cube trays or larger containers to freeze for up to 3 months.

split-pea stew

This wintry stew combines pears and parsnips that have been shredded on the large holes of a box grater with split, or dried, peas. Shredding foods, rather than chopping, is a great way to add nutrition to a dish without adding cooking time. Split peas need to be well cooked and well mashed for baby.

parsnip, 1

pear, 1

split peas, ½ cup, picked over and rinsed

water, 1 cup

Baby's Stock (page 44) or additional water, 1¼ cups

MAKES 1½ CUPS

● Peel parsnip and pear. Using the large holes of a box grater, shred enough of each to measure out ¼ cup.

● In a medium saucepan over medium heat, combine peas, water, stock (or additional water), parsnip, and pear. Cover and simmer until liquid is absorbed and peas are tender, 30–35 minutes. Be sure to cook peas well, until their texture is no longer grainy. Add more water or stock during cooking if needed to keep peas moist.

● Mash and combine with a wooden spoon, potato masher, or food processor to a consistency your baby can handle.

To store Refrigerate cooled split-pea stew in an airtight container for up to 3 days, or fill ice-cube trays or larger containers to freeze for up to 3 months.

lentils & lamb

extra-virgin olive oil, 1 tsp

fresh rosemary, 1 tsp minced

lamb shoulder or steak, ½ lb, cut into ½-inch pieces

Baby's Stock (page 44) or water, 1½ cups

lentils, ¼ cup, picked over and rinsed

MAKES 2 CUPS

• Heat oil in a saucepan over medium-high heat. Add rosemary and cook until fragrant, 30 seconds. Add lamb and stir frequently until browned. Add stock and lentils and bring to a boil. Reduce heat to maintain a simmer, cover, and cook for 15–20 minutes. Add more water or stock during cooking if needed to keep lentils moist.

• Pulse lamb and lentils in a food processor to a consistency your baby can handle.

To store Refrigerate cooled lentil-lamb mixture in an airtight container for up to 3 days, or fill ice-cube trays or larger containers to freeze for up to 1 month.

Rosemary adds memorable flavor and aroma to this hearty dish, rich in protein, iron and other minerals, B vitamins, and fiber. Lentils require less cooking time than other legumes (such as white or pinto beans), so this dish makes a quick and hearty staple for baby. Before pulsing or pureeing baby's portion, reserve some for the rest of the family, season with salt to taste, and serve over quinoa or couscous.

millet & zucchini medley

millet, ½ cup

Zucchini Puree
(page 23), ⅓ cup

Apple Puree
(page 27), 2 Tbsp

fresh basil, ¼ cup
finely chopped

MAKES 2 CUPS

- In a saucepan over high heat, bring 2 cups water to a boil. Add millet, cover, reduce heat to low, and cook until water is absorbed, 35–45 minutes.

- Fluff with a fork. You should have about 2 cups cooked millet. Divide millet evenly between 2 containers and refrigerate or freeze half for a later use. Stir zucchini and apple purees into remaining millet, let cool, and stir in basil just before serving.

Notes If you like, stir some of Baby's Turkey (page 35) into this dish as well, or tiny pieces of cut-up turkey from a grown-up's plate when baby has gotten good at gumming his food. To store, refrigerate cooled millet-zucchini mixture in an airtight container for up to 3 days, or fill ice-cube trays or larger containers to freeze for up to 3 months.

Basil gives this grain-and-veggie medley a fresh, summery flavor. Millet grains are naturally tiny, so it won't be long before your baby can graduate from Baby's Millet Cereal (page 34) to this unground version. This whole grain is a great staple for baby's diet while he is still too young for wheat, and the whole family can enjoy it in place of rice at dinnertime.

amaranth
& plum swirl

Mixing amaranth with fruit puree, such as plum, smooths its sticky texture. Amaranth is a seed that is treated like a grain because of its similarity in flavor and cooking. You'll hear it called a superfood because it offers a complete protein, a rarity in the plant world. Amaranth also offers a mother lode of minerals, including iron.

amaranth, 1/2 cup

**Plum Puree
(page 41),
1/4–1/2 cup, or
ripe plum, 1**

MAKES
1²/₃–1³/₄ CUPS

● In a saucepan over high heat, bring 1¹/₂ cups water to a boil. Add amaranth and bring back to a full, rolling boil. Stir, cover, and reduce heat to low. Cook, stirring occasionally with a whisk, until water is absorbed, 18–22 minutes. Amaranth will be translucent, thick, and sticky.

● Stir plum puree into amaranth. For older babies, simply pit, cut up, and mash a ripe plum and stir it into the amaranth.

To store Refrigerate cooled amaranth mixture in an airtight container for up to 3 days, or fill ice-cube trays or larger containers to freeze for up to 3 months.

squash
& quinoa pilaf

quinoa, ½ cup

extra-virgin olive oil, 2 Tbsp

Baby's Stock (page 44) or water, 1½ cups

summer squashes or zucchini, 2 small, coarsely shredded

ground cumin, ½ tsp

MAKES 2 CUPS

● In a saucepan, toss quinoa in 1 Tbsp of oil to coat. Add stock and bring to a boil over medium-high heat. Reduce heat to low, cover, and simmer for 20 minutes. Quinoa will be translucent.

● While quinoa is cooking, in a small frying pan over medium-high heat, heat remaining 1 Tbsp olive oil. Add squash and cumin and sauté until tender, 3–5 minutes.

● Remove quinoa from heat. Add squash to quinoa and mix thoroughly before serving.

To store Refrigerate cooled squash and quinoa pilaf in an airtight container for up to 3 days, or fill ice-cube trays or larger containers to freeze for up to 3 months.

Summer squash smooths the texture of quinoa (say "keen-wa"), a South American seed that, like amaranth, offers a complete protein. It has a nutty flavor and light texture, similar to couscous (which also is not a grain, but a pasta made from wheat). You can find quinoa in the bulk section of specialty grocers and health-food stores, or by mail order online. This pilaf makes a colorful stuffing for bell peppers or tomatoes for adults.

new textures

widening horizons

At this age, baby is a much more active participant in meals, trying to grab the spoon and feed herself, dropping food on the floor, spreading it in her hair. Your baby is now on the road to self-sufficiency at the table, so grin and bear the mess.

Let baby take the spoon sometimes and practice using it, or give her a second spoon to play with while you feed her. At this stage, mealtimes are becoming more chaotic and perhaps slower than before.

How Much & How Often?

Babies are very good at regulating their food intake if they are not pressured or even coaxed in any direction. Offer your child a variety of items from different food groups throughout the day, rather than worrying yet about "square meals."

Continue to offer breast milk or formula to baby as her primary source of nutrition. Once she's had her milk feed, let her eat as much food as she likes. When 3 meals a day no longer seem to satisfy baby's appetite, it's time to add snacks between meals. These should be healthy offerings, perhaps leftovers from a previous meal.

New Flavors

This age brings exciting new categories of foods to introduce to baby. At 9 months, try the easier-to-digest dairy products: yogurt and cheese. (Keep holding off on cow's milk until 1 year, however.) Hard-cooked egg yolks, separated from the more allergenic whites, are another new possibility. A wider range of legumes and meats are also on the menu, and all of these new foods are rich in protein, a boon for rapidly growing babies. You can also introduce some tropical fruits and blackberries, although you may wish to hold off on strawberries and raspberries until the first birthday. And baby can sample the savory alliums (onion family)—but if these gas-producing vegetables bother her, save them for later.

If allergies run in your family, remember to test these new foods one at a time for 3 days to make sure they agree with baby.

new opinions

It's a good thing that baby's menu is ever widening, because already her tastes may be changing, or she may be starting to exercise her own will. Your child may surprise you by suddenly rejecting foods that she formerly enjoyed.

You can try offering rejected foods in a new form, such as spread on bread or combined with other foods, and keep your patience and a bland expression. Baby might change her mind again tomorrow or next week, but a disapproving reaction from you (and baby is by now an expert in reading your reactions) may only encourage her in her refusals.

Super Chunky

As your baby grows and progresses, encourage her to try thicker and chunkier textures, while respecting what she is able to handle. At this stage, you'll use a food processor less and less, and a knife for chopping more and more. Instead of pureeing all the food you're serving baby, only puree half and coarsely mash or chop the rest, then combine. The recipes in this chapter more closely resemble "regular" food, and can easily feed an older child.

Self-Feeding

By the time your baby is 9 months old, she is old enough to start trying finger foods. Babies of this age are perfecting a new skill, the pincer grip (using thumb and index finger to pick things up), and food is the perfect object to practice on. In addition to spoon-feeding your baby's now chunkier food, spread some pieces on the high-chair tray. Some good items for baby to try picking up are finely diced cooked vegetables and soft fruit, bread spread with cheese or fruit purees and cut into small pieces, and foods that dissolve in the mouth, such as O-shaped oat cereals.

Now that baby is starting to feed herself, you might be tempted to run into the next room to take care of a task while she's busy in her high chair. However, keeping a close eye on your baby while she eats to prevent choking is more important than ever.

New Foods to Try

Let your 9- to 11-month-old try these wholesome new foods.

Legumes

dried beans (navy, pinto, garbanzo)
fava beans
lima beans
soybeans & tofu

Dairy

cheese
yogurt

Meat & Egg

beef
chicken
egg yolk (no whites)
pork
veal

baby's chicken

vegetable oil for greasing

boneless, skinless chicken thighs or breasts, 1/2–3/4 lb

MAKES
1 1/2–1 3/4 CUPS

- Preheat oven to 400°F. Set an oiled rack in an aluminum foil–lined baking pan. Put chicken on rack and bake, turning once, until opaque and no longer pink in the center, 12 minutes per side.

- Chop chicken coarsely, transfer to a dry food processor, and pulse until texture resembles small crumbs. As baby becomes more adept at chewing, cut chicken into small pieces.

To store Refrigerate chicken in an airtight container for 1–2 days, or freeze for up to 1 month.

Baking works well for mild, lean chicken breasts or flavorful, fattier, iron-rich thighs, while poaching is a simple way to cook fish and retain moisture. Pureed chicken can be mixed with purees and cereals for younger babies, while small chicken bits are great for toddlers to dip into yogurt or another wholesome dip.

baby's fish

Baby's Stock (page 44) or water, 1 cup or as needed

white fish fillets such as halibut, 1/2 lb

MAKES 1 CUP

- Heat stock to a simmer in a frying pan over medium-high heat. Add fish fillets. Stock should come about halfway up sides. Simmer, turning once, until opaque, 3–4 minutes per side. Fish should flake easily with a fork. Remove fish and let cool.

- Mash or flake fish to a consistency your baby can handle.

Notes If allergies run in the family, you may wish to delay introducing fish; consult your pediatrician. To store, refrigerate fish in an airtight container for 1–2 days.

baby's beef

lean ground beef, ½ lb

MAKES 1 CUP

- In a nonstick frying pan over medium heat, combine beef and ¼ cup water. Cook, breaking up meat and stirring constantly, until meat is cooked through and no longer pink, about 5 minutes. Let cool, then drain and reserve cooking juices.

- If needed, transfer beef to a food processor and pulse until texture resembles small crumbs, adding cooking juices as needed to moisten beef.

Notes If possible, buy a whole, lean rib or tenderloin cut and ask the butcher to grind it freshly for you. Lean cuts are higher in protein than the fattier cuts usually used for ground meat, and this way you may be more likely to get organic meat, and/or grass-fed beef, which is higher in healthful omega-3 fats than its corn-fed counterpart. To store, refrigerate cooled beef in an airtight container for 2–3 days, or freeze for up to 1 month.

Meat offers plenty of iron and protein, as well as B vitamins, for babies. Any ground meat—pork, lamb, or veal—can be cooked this way for baby. Meat purees are a bit bland and chalky for eating on their own. To make them more enticing, mix with vegetable or fruit purees.

oatmeal

ground cinnamon, 1/2 tsp

vanilla extract, 1 tsp

old-fashioned rolled oats, 1 cup

MAKES ABOUT 2 CUPS

A bowl of oatmeal is warming and nutritious, and lends itself to many flavorings and add-ins. This recipe calls for old-fashioned oats, which cook up with a good texture. Quick-cooking oats cook faster because they are cut up. Note that instant oatmeal packets tend to have sugar and other extraneous ingredients added.

● In a medium saucepan over high heat, combine 2 cups water, cinnamon, and vanilla and bring to a boil. Reduce heat to medium-low and stir in oats.

● When mixture begins to simmer, cover, turn off heat, and let stand until thick and creamy, about 15 minutes. Serve with breast milk, formula, or flavor options (below) stirred in.

Flavoring suggestions

Baby's purees make great additions to morning oatmeal. Here are some flavor, color, and texture variations for a 1/2-cup serving:

1 Tbsp mashed banana, plus 1 tsp Blueberry Sauce (page 38)

1 Tbsp Dried-Apricot Puree (page 39), plus 1 Tbsp diced pear (or, for older babies, mango)

2 Tbsp applesauce (or, for older babies, 1 Tbsp shredded apple), cut-up raisins, and a pinch of freshly grated nutmeg

toddler's brown rice

Brown rice remains an excellent staple food for baby as he grows, but as he reaches toddlerhood he'll be ready for the whole-grain version instead of the ground mush (page 22). Use as a side dish, as a bed for recipes like Baby's Curry (page 85), or as an ingredient in recipes such as the Toddler Burrito (page 120).

brown rice, 1 cup

Baby's Stock (page 44), low-sodium broth, or water, 2 cups

fruit or vegetable puree of choice (optional)

MAKES 3–4 CUPS

● In a medium saucepan over high heat, combine rice and stock and bring to a boil. Stir, reduce heat to low, cover, and cook until stock is absorbed and rice is tender, about 40 minutes. Remove pan from heat and let sit, covered, for 5 minutes.

● If needed, pulse rice in a food processor, adding 1/4 cup water to prevent sticking, or pass rice through a food mill fitted with a coarse disk. The rice will be very sticky, but can be blended with a fruit or vegetable puree to smooth it.

Notes You can make rice using stock or broth in place of water for extra flavor and nutrition. If purchasing prepared broth, be sure to choose the low- or no-sodium kind, to give yourself more control over the seasoning and amount of salt in baby's food.

The recipes in this chapter begin to add salt to baby's food. An advantage to preparing your baby's food yourself is that you are able to control the amount of salt you use. As part of a diet low in high-sodium processed foods, a pinch of salt brings out flavor in food and supplies sodium, a necessary nutrient. Iodized salt also supplies iodine, another essential nutrient. However, if you feed your baby ready-made foods or tidbits from your own plate, you are likely giving him foods that contain plenty of sodium, so you may wish to omit salt in the foods you prepare specially for him.

Refrigerate cooked rice in an airtight container for up to 5 days.

hard-cooked egg

eggs, 6 large

MAKES 6 HARD-
COOKED EGGS

- Put eggs in a pot and add enough water to cover by 1 inch. Bring to a rolling boil over medium-high heat. As soon as water reaches a boil, remove from heat, cover pot, and let stand for 14 minutes.

- Drain water and rinse eggs under running cold water to stop the cooking. Tap each egg all over to break the shell, then peel. Shells peel most easily from the rounder end (where there is an air space).

Notes Gray or green color around egg yolks is a sign of overcooking but is not harmful. To store, refrigerate hard-cooked eggs in their shells for up to 1 week. If allergies run in your family, you may wish to delay introducing eggs; consult your pediatrician.

baby's egg yolks

hard-cooked egg yolk (above), 1

plain whole-milk yogurt, 1 Tbsp

avocado, 1 Tbsp mashed

bread, 1 slice

MAKES 2½ TBSP
SPREAD

- In a small mixing bowl, mash yolk with the back of a fork. Add yogurt and avocado and mash together until smooth.

- Spread onto bread and cut into small dice or strips for baby to serve himself.

Notes To store egg yolk mixture, refrigerate in an airtight container for 1–2 days. If you haven't yet introduced wheat to your baby, look for bread made from other grains. Wheatless rye bread is widely available, and you may be able to find breads made from millet, spelt, kamut, teff, rice, or potato flour.

Egg are densely nutritious, rich in protein, calcium, vitamins, and minerals. Most pediatricians recommend feeding only egg yolks during the first year, as the whites are especially allergenic. Hard cooking is the best way to separate an egg for a baby that is not yet eating the whites. Note that even with a careful separation of white and yolk, some white may remain on the yolk

barley &
mushrooms

**pearl barley,
¹/₂ cup**

**unsalted butter,
1 Tbsp**

**garlic, 1 clove,
minced**

**cremini
mushrooms,
6 oz, finely
chopped (2 cups)**

**Baby's Stock
(page 44) or
low-sodium
broth, 1 cup**

salt, ¹/₄ tsp

pepper, ¹/₈ tsp

**thyme, ¹/₈ tsp
dried, or ¹/₂ tsp
minced fresh**

MAKES ABOUT
2¹/₂ CUPS

● In a dry saucepan over medium heat, toast barley, stirring often, until it starts to brown, about 3 minutes. Transfer to a mixing bowl.

● In same saucepan over medium heat, melt butter. Add garlic and cook until aromatic, about 1 minute. Stir in mushrooms and cook until they release their liquid and become tender, about 3 minutes. Stir in barley, stock, ¹/₃ cup water, salt, pepper, and thyme. Bring to a boil over high heat, reduce heat to medium-low, cover, and simmer until barley is tender, 30–35 minutes.

● Depending on your baby's age and chewing ability, serve whole, pass through a food mill, or puree in a food processor, adding water as needed to make a coarse puree.

To store Refrigerate puree in an airtight container for up to 3 days.

The mushrooms in this dish provide baby with plenty of B vitamins, iron, and other minerals, and wholesome barley can be a welcome change of pace from the usual rice side dish the rest of your family may expect. The mushrooms you choose will alter the richness and flavor of this dish. You may even want to try a mix of exotic mushrooms, such as portobello, chanterelle, and shiitake.

The recipes on this page pack a nutritional punch and may well become staples in your baby's diet. Avocados are a superfood, full of protein, healthy fat, fiber, B vitamins, and zinc. The yogurt smoothie is filling, versatile (it can be made with just about any fruit), and is an excellent source of protein for growing children.

avocado-cheese spread

avocado, ½ large (about ⅓ cup)

cream cheese, ⅓ cup

bread, 1 slice

MAKES ⅔ CUP

● In a small mixing bowl, mash avocado with a fork until smooth. Add cream cheese and mash together.

● Spread onto bread and cut into small dice or strips for baby to serve herself.

Notes For information on wheatless bread, see Notes on Baby's Egg Yolks, page 63. To store, refrigerate in an airtight container for up to 1 day. Spread will discolor slightly with storage but this is not harmful. Stirring will return it to a pale green color.

fruity smoothie

frozen banana, 1, cut into 2-inch chunks

frozen or fresh peaches, 1 cup peeled and sliced

plain whole-milk yogurt, ½ cup

flaxseed meal, 1 Tbsp

MAKES ABOUT 2½ CUPS

● Put banana, peaches, yogurt, and flaxseed meal in a blender and blend until smooth.

Notes As baby gets older, try making the smoothie with berries or tropical fruits such as mango, pineapple, or papaya. The use of frozen fruit rather than fresh or thawed means there's no need for ice, which can be too cold for small children. To freeze bananas, simply peel, wrap in waxed paper, and store in freezer bags in the freezer for up to 3 months. This is a good trick to remember when you have a bunch of overripe bananas on hand. You can also use room-temperature fruit for kids who don't like their drinks too cold. To store, refrigerate in an airtight container for up to 2 days.

parsnip & broccoli gratin

unsalted butter for greasing

parsnips, 6 medium, peeled

Baby's Stock (page 44) or low-sodium broth, 1/2 cup

Whipped Cauliflower made with broccoli (page 36), 1 cup

Parmesan cheese, 1/2 cup grated

MAKES FOUR 3 1/2-INCH GRATINS

● Preheat oven to 375°F. Butter four 3 1/2-inch ramekins.

● Using a mandoline slicer or chef's knife, carefully slice parsnips into rounds 1/4 inch thick. Layer 1/2 cup parsnips in each ramekin. Pour 2 Tbsp stock over each ramekin. Divide broccoli puree among ramekins, spreading it to cover parsnips. Top each ramekin with 2 Tbsp Parmesan cheese.

● Place ramekins on a baking sheet and bake until gratins are bubbly and cheese starts to look golden, about 25 minutes. Let cool before feeding gratin to baby.

To store Wrap and refrigerate ramekins for up to 3 days.

Preparing this gratin in individual ramekins makes the dish especially appealing to both children and adults. It might even convince a stubborn toddler to eat her broccoli, which is off the chart in vitamins C and K and contains a long list of other nutrients. Just make sure that the ramekin is completely cooled before bringing it to the table for baby.

finger foods for babies

By the age of 9 months, baby will likely let you know he is interested in feeding himself by grabbing the spoon and picking food up in his hands. It will be a while yet before he is able to wield a spoon on his own, but he can certainly learn to eat with his hands now. At mealtime, alongside any food you're spoon-feeding him, offer small pieces of tender foods that he can pick up himself. Note that babies do not need teeth in order to eat finger foods. They can mash foods very efficiently with their gums. However, to begin with, you should choose foods that are very soft or that dissolve easily.

As baby becomes comfortable with finger foods, they can start to make up more of his meal. Scatter a few pieces of 2 or 3 different foods on baby's high-chair tray so that he can choose. You can add more tidbits as baby eats them. Serving too much food to a baby at once can be overwhelming to him and can inspire throwing and smearing.

Fruits & Vegetables

Choose produce that is naturally soft, or steam it until tender.

- Ripe soft fruit: plums, pears, peaches

- Chunks of ripe banana or avocado rolled in crushed oat cereal

- Finely diced cooked apples or Asian pears

- Finely diced well-cooked vegetables: carrots, broccoli, tender green beans, squash

Meat & Dairy

These high-protein foods are in demand among rapidly growing babies.

- Pasteurized semisoft cheese, cut into tiny dice

- Rye bread smeared with goat cheese or liverwurst and cut into little pieces or strips

- Finely diced cooked chicken and turkey

Grains & Legumes

Grains and legumes provide energy for busy babies learning to crawl and move around independently.

- Small pieces of rice cake
- Pieces or strands of well-cooked rice pasta

- Low-sugar O-shaped oat or rice cereal

- Halved or mashed well-cooked (or canned) beans

snacks for toddlers

As baby nears 1 year and becomes more and more active with crawling, pulling himself up, cruising, and perhaps walking, snacks between meals become a major source of fuel. Often baby's new independence means he will not want to sit still for very long to eat. However, despite any protests, you should be sure to keep him in his high chair when eating, whether it's a full meal or a quick snack. This will help prevent choking, help teach good dining habits, and help contain the nearly inevitable mealtime mess.

Think of snacks as miniature meals rather than sugary or salty processed items from the grocery store. The easiest snack is a few bites of a leftover meal. Below are wholesome snack suggestions for a young toddler nearing 1 year.

Fruits & Vegetables

These foods are digestible and nutritious, and usually agree with babies.

- Cut-up grapes and strawberries; small pieces of melon, papaya, pineapple, and kiwifruit

- Steamed peas or *edamame* (soybeans)

Meat & Dairy

If your child has allergic tendencies, use caution when introducing egg and fish, and limit tuna to once a week for all children.

- String cheese peeled into thin strips

- Finely diced cooked beet and lamb

- Pieces of omelet, frittata, and quiche

- Tiny tuna or egg salad sandwiches made with cocktail bread

Grains & Legumes

If your child has allergic tendencies, use caution when introducing wheat

- Muffins and scones

- Cut-up wheat bagel smeared with hummus

- Whole-wheat crackers smeared with fruit puree

- Cut-up pieces of pancakes, crepes, or waffles

- Cut-up pieces of cooked pasta (penne, bow ties, and elbow macaroni)

roasted red pepper & goat cheese puree

**red bell pepper,
1 large**

**pasteurized fresh
goat cheese,
1½ oz**

MAKES 1 CUP

● Preheat broiler. Line a roasting pan with aluminum foil. Place whole pepper on pan and roast, turning every 3 minutes, until evenly charred and blackened on all sides, 12–15 minutes.

● Remove pan from oven, put pepper in a covered container, and let sit until cool enough to handle. (The steam inside the container will loosen the skin.)

● Using your fingers or a pearing knife, peel off skin. Cut pepper in half lengthwise and remove seeds and stem. Cut halves in half again lengthwise and puree in a food processor until smooth. Additional liquid will not be needed. Spoon goat cheese into processor and process with pepper puree until well blended and creamy.

To store Refrigerate puree in an airtight container for up to 3 days.

Red, orange, and yellow bell peppers are ripe and sweet. All three colors are high in vitamin C and beta-carotene. This recipe adds protein-rich goat cheese to the peppers, yielding a creamy puree that is delicious by itself or can be used as a sauce for rice noodles or as a dip for steamed vegetable sticks.

confetti slaw

In this recipe, produce takes center stage with a bright, vitamin-rich mix of colors and flavors that will entice children and adults alike. For maximum nutritional benefit, choose organic zucchini and leave the skin on. When your baby is old enough to handle it, leave the apple skin on as well.

red bell pepper, ½ large, stemmed, seeded, and coarsely chopped

balsamic vinegar, ½ tsp

extra-virgin olive oil, ½ tsp

zucchini, 1 medium

Fuji apple, 1 small, peeled, halved, and cored

MAKES 1½ CUPS

● Put pepper in a food processor with vinegar and oil. Pulse until pepper is pureed.

● Using the large holes on a box grater, shred zucchini and apple. Put shredded zucchini and apple in a clean, dry dish towel, hold over a bowl, and gently squeeze out excess liquid. (Reserve the juice for baby's cup or add it to plain yogurt.) Put zucchini and apple in a medium mixing bowl and toss with a fork to separate.

● Add bell pepper mixture to shredded mixture and toss to mix.

To store Refrigerate slaw in an airtight container for up to 3 days.

red beans & rice

dried small red beans, 1/2 cup

olive-oil spray

precooked chicken sausage, 3 oz, chopped

ground cumin, 1/4 tsp

fresh flat-leaf parsley, 1/2 tsp minced

Toddler's Brown Rice (page 62), 1 cup

MAKES 3 CUPS

● Pick over and rinse beans. For a quick soak, combine in a saucepan with 2 cups water and bring to a rapid boil over medium-high heat. Boil for 2 minutes, remove from heat, cover, and let stand for 1 hour. Drain and rinse beans.

● To cook beans, combine 2 fresh cups water and beans in a saucepan over medium-high heat. Bring to a boil. Reduce heat to maintain a simmer, cover, and simmer until beans are tender, about 1 1/2 hours. Add more water if needed to keep beans from drying out.

● Spray a sauté pan with olive oil and heat over medium heat. Add sausage. Sprinkle cumin and parsley over sausage, stir, and cook until sausage is heated through, 6–8 minutes or as directed on package.

● Stir together beans, chicken sausage, and rice. Depending on your baby's age and chewing ability, serve beans and rice whole as finger food; mash together with a fork; or pulse in a food processor, adding water as needed to make a coarse puree.

To store Refrigerate beans and rice in an airtight container for up to 3 days.

When choosing dried beans for this dish, choose small red beans over dark red kidney beans. They mash up into a smoother texture. If pressed for time, use rinsed canned beans. This dish includes chicken sausage for savory flavor, but it's also useful to know that even without the meat, the combination of beans and rice gives baby a complete protein (that is, all 8 essential amino acids our bodies require).

succotash

unsalted butter, 1 Tbsp

lima or butter beans, fresh shelled or thawed frozen, 1 cup

corn kernels, fresh or thawed frozen, 1 cup

paprika, 1/4 tsp

salt, 1/4 tsp

Baby's Stock (page 44) or low-sodium broth, 1/2 cup

MAKES 2 CUPS

● In a medium saucepan over medium heat, melt butter. Add beans, corn, paprika, and salt and sauté until aromatic, about 3 minutes. Stir in stock, cover, and cook until vegetables are tender, about 10 minutes.

● Depending on your baby's age and chewing ability, pass succotash through a food mill or process briefly in a food processor to make a coarse mince.

Notes Little fingers will enjoy the whole beans and kernels—but note that corn kernels can be a choking hazard for younger babies, and families with allergies may wish to delay introducing corn until baby turns 1. When baby reaches 1 year, you can also add some diced tomato for color and additional vitamins. Refrigerate succotash in an airtight container for up to 3 days.

Over the centuries, this bean dish evolved from a simple Native American recipe featuring corn and other New World ingredients to a Southern classic soaked in bacon grease. Here, it gets a healthful makeover. High in fiber, iron, and minerals, baby lima beans are small, flat, greenish beans with a buttery flavor and creamy texture.

edamame & yogurt puree

Nutrient-dense soybeans are an excellent meatless source of protein and contain heathy fats, numerous vitamins and minerals, and fiber. Here, creamy yogurt balances the texture of the edamame. When she is older, your child may enjoy the soybeans simply steamed in their pods, lightly salted, and eaten right out of the shell.

edamame (soybeans), fresh or frozen, ½ cup shelled

plain whole-milk yogurt, ¼ cup

fresh flat-leaf parsley or mint, ¼ tsp minced

MAKES ½ CUP

● Bring 1 inch water to a boil in a pot. If using fresh soybeans, place them in a steamer basket, set in pot, cover tightly, and steam until tender, about 20 minutes. If using frozen soybeans, follow package directions.

● Puree edamame in a food processor until smooth, stopping once to scrape down sides of workbowl. Puree will have a pastelike consistency. Add yogurt and process until creamy and smooth.

● Stir in parsley and serve.

Notes If allergies run in your family, you may wish to delay introducing soy; consult your pediatrician. To store, refrigerate in an airtight container for up to 3 days, or freeze fresh edamame puree before adding yogurt for up to 3 months.

silken tofu & peach puree

silken tofu, 1 cup

Peach Puree (page 41), 1/4 cup

toasted wheat germ, 1/2 tsp (optional)

MAKES 1 1/4 CUPS

- In a medium mixing bowl, whisk tofu until creamy. Divide tofu among four 3 1/2-inch ramekins.

- Place 1 Tbsp peach puree in the center of each ramekin. Swirl puree into tofu with the spoon handle to make a pretty pattern.

- Sprinkle each ramekin with 1/8 tsp toasted wheat germ, if using.

Notes If allergies run in your family, you may wish to delay introducing soy and wheat; consult your pediatrician. To store, refrigerate in an airtight container for up to 3 days.

Baby's summer peach puree adds a touch of alluring flavor and color to this recipe featuring beneficial soy in a fermented form: creamy silken tofu. Once your baby is eating wheat, top this dish with toasted wheat germ for a nutty and crunchy appeal. This is an easy dessert or breakfast option for any age.

root veggie medley

Roasting brings out the rich, earthy colors and flavors of nutritious root vegetables. And rosemary, like many other herbs, brings more than just delicious aroma and flavor to this dish. It's rich in antioxidants, compounds found in many plants that help boost the immune system and fight disease.

sweet potato or yam, 1

parsnips, 2

carrots, 2

extra-virgin olive oil, 2 Tbsp

fresh rosemary, 2 tsp minced

salt, 1/4 tsp

pepper, 1/4 tsp

MAKES ABOUT 2 CUPS

● Preheat oven to 400°F. Peel sweet potato, parsnips, and carrots. Using a mandoline or chef's knife, carefully slice vegetables into rounds 1/2 inch thick. Cut sweet potato rounds into quarters or as needed to roughly match the size of the parsnips and carrots.

● Put vegetables in a ceramic or glass baking dish. Drizzle with oil, sprinkle with rosemary, salt, and pepper, and toss to coat. Roast until vegetables are tender, 15–20 minutes.

● Depending on your baby's age and chewing ability, mash part of the cooked vegetable medley and puree part in a food processor and then combine for a variety of textures. Or, simply cut vegetable pieces smaller to accommodate little mouths.

To store Refrigerate in an airtight container for up to 3 days.

minced pork & pear

When baby can gum his food well and has begun to enjoy thicker textures, meats become more appealing. Mild pork and sweet fruit always make a good combination, and pork is bred so lean nowadays that it's a great source of protein. Use any color and type of pear you'd like, or, in summertime, try plums.

Baby's Stock (page 44) or low-sodium broth, ½ cup

pork cutlets or boneless chops, ½ lb, cut into ½-inch cubes

pear, ½, peeled and chopped

nutmeg, ⅛ tsp freshly grated

MAKES 1 CUP

- In an 8-inch frying pan over medium heat, bring stock to a simmer. Add pork and spread out in stock. The liquid should not cover pork; pork will float. Simmer until pork is no longer pink, about 3 minutes. Remove with a slotted spoon.

- In a small mixing bowl, toss pear with nutmeg. Add pear to stock in pan, cover, and simmer over medium heat until soft, about 3 minutes, depending on ripeness. Drain and reserve cooking liquid.

- Transfer pork to a food processor and pulse until minced, about 12 times.

- Transfer pears to a small mixing bowl and mash with the back of a fork. Add pork to pears and stir to combine. Add cooking liquid to adjust moistness, if needed.

To store Refrigerate in an airtight container for up to 3 days.

chicken & vegetable kebabs

skinless, boneless chicken breast, 1 large (³/₄ lb), cut into 1¹/₂-inch cubes

low-sodium soy sauce, 3 Tbsp

canola oil, 1 Tbsp

brown sugar, ¹/₂ tsp

ground ginger, ¹/₄ tsp

summer squash or zucchini, 1 medium

red and/or orange bell pepper(s), 1 medium or 8 miniature

brown or white mushrooms, 8

MAKES 4 SKEWERS

● Put chicken in a large glass dish. In a small mixing bowl, whisk together soy sauce, oil, sugar, and ginger to make a marinade. Reserving 1 Tbsp marinade in a small bowl, pour marinade over chicken. Cover and refrigerate for at least 30 minutes or up to 4 hours. Meanwhile, soak 4 wooden skewers in cold water for at least 30 minutes.

● Preheat a broiler, or prepare a grill for direct grilling over high heat. Cut squash into 1-inch rounds. Stem and seed pepper(s) and cut into ¹/₂-inch squares. Place squash, pepper(s), and mushrooms in a medium mixing bowl. Drizzle with reserved 1 Tbsp marinade and toss to coat evenly.

● Drain skewers. Thread chicken and vegetables onto skewers, alternating as desired. If broiling, place kebabs on a lightly greased baking sheet or broiler pan. Broil or grill until browned on first side, 5–6 minutes. Turn and broil on second side until browned and chicken is cooked through, 4–6 minutes.

To store Refrigerate in an airtight container for up to 3 days.

This all-purpose recipe can be adjusted to serve any age and taste—not just baby. Choose any mix of colors, vegetables, and meats to suit your family's preferences. If needed, you can puree the chicken and vegetables for younger babies. For toddlers, chop them into small pieces they can pick up. Serve this with Millet & Zucchini Medley (page 51) or with Polenta (page 94).

blackberry &
ricotta parfait

**blackberries,
1 cup, plus extra
for garnish**

**ricotta cheese,
½ cup**

**nutmeg, ⅛ tsp
freshly grated**

**ground
cinnamon, ⅛ tsp**

MAKES 1½ CUPS

- Puree blackberries in a food processor until smooth. There will be seeds in the puree. To remove them, put puree in a fine-mesh sieve over a small mixing bowl and push puree through sieve with a rubber spatula.

- In a small mixing bowl, stir together ricotta, nutmeg, and cinnamon. In a dessert cup, alternate layers of blackberry puree and ricotta mixture. Finish with a halved berry on top.

Notes Blackberries are less allergenic than strawberries or raspberries, but if allergies run in your family, you may wish to delay introducing all berries; consult your pediatrician. To store parfait, cover tightly and refrigerate for up to 2 days.

This parfait is a lovely and healthful way to elevate berries into a special treat. The layering of colors and flavors works well with a single berry such as blackberry or blueberry, or, for older babies, raspberry or strawberry. You can also try a mixture of berries. The ricotta smooths and adds richness to the sometimes-tart berries, and the spices lend a bit of sweetness.

baby's dal

This version of the savory Indian dish combining spices, vegetables, and red lentils is not too spicy for young palates. Red lentils are smaller than green or brown ones and cook fairly quickly. They are an excellent source of protein, folate, iron and other minerals, and fiber for young eaters.

red lentils, 1/3 cup

baby carrots, 12

small red potatoes, 3

green onions, 2 Tbsp chopped

Baby's Stock (page 44) or low-sodium broth, 2 cups, or as needed

curry powder, ground coriander, ground turmeric, and ground cumin, 1/4 tsp *each*

MAKES ABOUT 3 CUPS

- Pick over lentils, discarding misshapen ones. Rinse and drain.

- Finely chop carrots and potatoes.

- In a saucepan over medium-high heat, combine all ingredients. Cover, reduce heat to medium, and simmer until vegetables are tender, about 20 minutes. Stir every 5 minutes and check to make sure stock is not all absorbed. Add more if necessary.

- Depending on your baby's age and chewing ability, serve whole, mash with a potato masher, or puree in a food processor, adding water as needed to make a coarse puree.

To store Refrigerate dal in an airtight container for up to 3 days.

baby's curry

skinless, boneless chicken breast, 1 large (³/₄ lb)

cornstarch, 1 tsp

canola or grape seed oil, 1 Tbsp

zucchini and/or other summer squash, 1 cup diced

coconut milk, ¹/₂ cup

Baby's Stock (page 44) or low-sodium broth, ¹/₂ cup

red curry paste or mild curry powder, 1 tsp

fresh basil, 2 Tbsp chopped

MAKES ABOUT 3 CUPS

- Cut chicken into narrow strips.

- Put cornstarch in a small bowl and stir in 1 Tbsp water.

- Heat oil in a wok over medium-high heat. Add chicken and stir-fry for about 2 minutes. Remove chicken and set aside.

- Add zucchini, coconut milk, stock, and curry paste to wok and bring to a boil. Reduce heat to medium, cover, and simmer until zucchini is tender, 6–7 minutes. Return chicken to wok and add basil. Stir cornstarch mixture to recombine and add to wok. Cook, stirring constantly, until sauce has thickened and chicken is cooked through, about 2 minutes.

- When dishing baby's portion, cut the chicken into small pieces.

Notes To give baby's curry a Thai flavor, look for mild jarred red curry paste prepared without shrimp or shellfish. Note that green curry paste is hotter than red and should not be substituted here. If red curry paste is not available, choose mild Indian curry powder. To store, refrigerate curry in an airtight container for up to 3 days.

This is a simple one-wok meal the whole family can enjoy together. If you do not have a wok, cook it in a large saucepan. The coconut milk lends the right amount of sweetness to please little palates. Its fat content is great for babies, but if adults are sharing, feel free to use light coconut milk. Serve over Toddler's Brown Rice (page 62).

little trees

Roasting broccoli and cauliflower florets gives them a golden color with rich caramelized brown bits on top and brings out a delicious nutty flavor. If desired, stand "trees" in a bed of mashed sweet potatoes to create a tasty (and supremely nutritious) little forest of broccoli trees and impress your youngster.

broccoli and/or cauliflower, 4 cups slender florets

extra-virgin olive oil, 2 Tbsp

sea salt, ¼ tsp

pepper

MAKES ABOUT 2 CUPS

- Preheat oven to 400°F. Make sure florets are trimmed to a uniform size.

- In a large mixing bowl, toss florets with oil, salt, and pepper to taste. Put vegetables in a ceramic or glass baking dish. Roast, stirring once, until broccoli is tender-crisp and browned in spots, 25–30 minutes.

- Serve hot or warm. Depending on your baby's age and chewing ability, keep "trees" whole, slice them lengthwise, or coarsely chop.

Notes Serve with lemon wedges for diners over age 1, if desired. To store, refrigerate florets in an airtight container for up to 3 days.

9 to 11 months

rice noodles primavera

This recipe features all the fresh green vegetables of spring and bright-flavored dill, but you can add any vegetables or herbs your baby enjoys. This is a fun dish for baby to practice his pincer grip on and feed himself. Rice pasta is a good introduction to noodles because they don't contain the common allergens that are found in most pasta: wheat and eggs.

asparagus,
¼ cup chopped

fresh or frozen peas, ¼ cup

fresh or frozen artichoke hearts, ⅓ cup chopped

rice pasta, ¼ lb

unsalted butter, 1 Tbsp

Zucchini Puree (page 23), 2 Tbsp

fresh dill, 1 tsp minced

MAKES 4 CUPS

● Select a pot with a steamer basket insert and fill two-thirds full with water. Bring to a boil over medium-high heat. Have ready asparagus, peas, and artichoke hearts in steamer basket. Add pasta to pot and, after 4 minutes of cooking, insert steamer basket of vegetables in pot. Cover and cook until both pasta and vegetables are just tender, about 5 minutes.

● Remove steamer basket from pot. Drain pasta, reserving 1 Tbsp cooking liquid, and put pasta in a large bowl. Cut pasta noodles into baby bite-sized pieces with kitchen shears. Add asparagus, peas, and artichoke hearts to pasta. Add reserved cooking liquid, butter, zucchini puree, and dill to bowl and stir to combine.

● Depending on your baby's age and chewing ability, serve whole or mash the peas, asparagus, and artichoke hearts with a fork.

Notes If you don't have a multipot with a basket insert, you can use 2 pots, one to cook the pasta and one to steam the vegetables. To store, refrigerate noodles in an airtight container for up to 3 days.

asparagus spears with feta

**asparagus,
1 bunch
(about 1 lb)**

olive oil, 2 Tbsp

**kosher or rock
salt, 2 tsp**

**feta cheese,
1/3 cup crumbled**

MAKES ABOUT
2 CUPS

● Preheat oven to 400°F. Line a 9 by 12 inch baking pan with aluminum foil.

● Snap off woody ends of asparagus spears and place spears in pan. Drizzle with oil, sprinkle with salt, and roll to coat. Roast until spears are tender, 8–10 minutes. Remove from oven and sprinkle with cheese.

● Depending on your baby's age and chewing ability, let her nibble on the spears, cut them into pieces, or mash them coarsely with a fork.

To store Refrigerate asparagus and feta in an airtight container for up to 3 days.

This is a great dish for the whole family. Roasting asparagus brings out a sweet flavor that goes over surprisingly well even with little vegetable-phobes. You'd swear this asparagus was cooked on the grill, but using the oven is much easier, with less preparation and cleanup. Serve hot with grilled meats or as a cold side for a picnic or brunch.

real meals

a world of flavor

Congratulations. Even if he's not quite walking yet, your child has arrived at toddlerhood! By now, he is likely eating a wide variety of foods and coarser textures. He's probably more interested than ever in getting tidbits from your plate, or feeding his food to you.

Perhaps he is starting to home in on some favorite foods and to refuse others that he previously enjoyed. Keep offering a variety of foods, even if they are rejected. A good strategy now is to offer a couple of familiar things along with a new item. The more flavors your child experiences at a young age, the more likely he is to come back to eating a wide range of foods later, following a nearly inevitable picky phase.

How Often & How Much?

At this age, your child will be constantly on the go, moving, climbing, and exploring. He needs a constant supply of fuel to support his high energy level. Expect to be feeding him 3 meals a day plus 2 or 3 healthy snacks. Try making a snack tray in the morning, putting various cut-up items in an ice-cube tray for baby to pick and choose from throughout the day at snack time or mealtime.

At this age, roughly 40 to 50 percent of your child's diet should still come from fat. For growth and brain development, offer plenty of fat- and protein-rich foods, such as whole milk, cheese, yogurt, meat, poultry, eggs, fish, and avocados. (If you wish to feed a vegetarian diet, consult your pediatrician to ensure that you meet your child's nutritional needs.) For energy, offer complex carbohydrates such as beans and whole-grain breads and pasta.

New Skills

At this age, your child can handle a sippy cup pretty well by himself; you can retire the bottle now. He is less skillful with a spoon. Before about 18 months, toddlers have difficulty scooping food from a bowl and then changing the angle of their wrists to insert the spoon in their mouths. Keep letting him practice with the spoon, especially with sticky foods like polenta or oatmeal.

family meals

The recipes in this chapter can be enjoyed by the whole family. At this point, you don't need to make special meals for baby. Your child can eat most of the same dishes as mom, dad, and siblings: just chop or mash his portion to make it manageable.

The sociability of eating together as a family is a good experience for your child to have now. Try to sit down and eat your own meal, or at least a snack, at the same time as your child. Pull his high chair up to the table and talk to your toddler about the food you are eating or your day. Families that share at least one meal together around the table find that it keeps them closer and more in tune—it's often the only time in a busy day when a real conversation can happen.

Toddler Quirks

Towards 18 months, your child may start to develop some curious ideas about food. He might want whole pieces of bread or other foods, not "broken" or cut up, or only foods of a certain color. He may become obsessed with one particular food for some period of time. Or, he may simply refuse everything. Be considerate of your little one's desires at mealtimes, but avoid catering to imperious demands. If your child learns that he can send his dinner back and have something else specially made, he will surely push for this, making his parents into short-order cooks. This is one area where kind firmness and absolute consistency will help.

Variety & Choice

Be patient and keep offering variety. Let him see you enjoying the same wholesome foods you're giving him. Offer a few different dishes or items at each meal, including one you know he'll eat (if possible) and let him decide what to eat and how much. If you are worried about his food intake, keep the big picture in mind: aim for balanced meals over the course of a week, rather than during any particular mealtime or day. One day he might eat fruit and refuse vegetables; the next day he might relish his vegetables. If he eats just a few foods, offer ones that are rich in fat, calories, and nutrients, especially milk.

New Foods to Try

Now that baby is 1, almost everything is on the menu.

Vegetables

spinach (cooked)
eggplant

Fruits

fig
grapefruit
kiwifruit
mango
melon
orange & other citrus
papaya
raspberry
strawberry
tomato
watermelon

Dairy, Meat, Seafood & Egg

cow's milk
beef
whole egg
fish

Other

honey

polenta

Polenta (cornmeal) and bulgur (cracked wheat) can be enjoyed with sweet or savory stir-ins. Blended with fruit and cream, polenta makes a hearty breakfast staple. Or, add Parmesan to make a dinner-time side dish. Bulgur, a staple in Middle Eastern cooking, can be drizzled with olive oil or blended with yogurt and fruit.

salt, $\frac{1}{2}$ **tsp**

polenta, $\frac{1}{2}$ **cup**

unsalted butter, 1 tsp

grated Parmesan cheese or cream and fruit for serving

MAKES 1½ CUPS

● In a saucepan over medium-high heat, bring 2 cups water and salt to a boil. Reduce heat to medium and slowly whisk in polenta. Cook, stirring frequently with a whisk to prevent lumps and sticking, until polenta is thickened, no longer tastes grainy, and has absorbed all the water, 15–30 minutes. Cooking time will vary from brand to brand; consult manufacturer's instructions. Be cautious, as polenta will bubble, pop, and spit if heat is too high. Stir in butter and let cool before serving.

● Serve with a handful of grated Parmesan stirred in, or blended with cream and diced fresh fruit.

To store Refrigerate in an airtight container for up to 4 days.

bulgur

bulgur wheat, $\frac{1}{2}$ **cup**

golden raisins, $\frac{1}{2}$ **cup, chopped**

boiling water, 1 cup

olive oil or yogurt and fruit for serving

MAKES 2 CUPS

● In a glass bowl, combine bulgur and raisins. Add boiling water. Cover tightly and let sit until water has been absorbed, about 1 hour.

● Serve bulgur drizzled with a little oil, or mixed with yogurt and diced fresh fruit.

Notes Bulgur is a form of wheat, so when introducing it for the first time remember to feed it on 3 consecutive days and watch or reactions. To store, refrigerate bulgur in an airtight container for up to 4 days.

cheese sauce

**unsalted butter,
1 Tbsp**

**unbleached flour,
2 Tbsp**

**whole milk,
1¼ cups**

**Swiss or sharp
Cheddar cheese,
½ cup shredded**

**nutmeg, ⅛ tsp
freshly grated**

MAKES ABOUT
1½ CUPS

● In a small saucepan over medium-low heat, melt butter. Add flour and cook, stirring with a whisk, until a thick paste forms, about 1 minute. Whisk in milk, a little at a time. Whisk continuously until the sauce bubbles and becomes creamy and thick, 5–7 minutes. Remove pan from heat and stir in cheese and nutmeg.

Notes Feel free to use any cheese your family enjoys in this sauce. Other cheese that melt well and taste great are mozzarella and Gruyère. To store, refrigerate cheese sauce in an airtight container for up to 3 days.

pureed spinach

**spinach,
1 bunch fresh or
10 oz frozen**

MAKES ABOUT
1 CUP

● If using fresh spinach, separate leaves and trim off stems. Fill a basin or large bowl with lukewarm water, plunge leaves into water, and swish thoroughly. The silt and sand will sink to the bottom, leaving you with clean leaves.

● Bring 1 inch water to a boil in a pot. Put spinach in a steamer basket, set in pot, cover tightly, and steam until spinach is wilted and bright green, 2–3 minutes. Rinse spinach under running cold water. Drain, squeeze, and puree in a food processor until smooth.

To store Refrigerate spinach in an airtight container for up to 3 days.

Some kids won't eat their veggies without a little encouragement. Here are two secret weapons for parents. First, a simple, creamy, versatile cheese sauce that is good mixed with Pureed Spinach (left) or drizzled onto chunky vegetables (or chicken, fish, or pasta). Second, a puree of spinach that can be stirred into other dishes to boost the nutritional content. Try it in Hidden Veggie Sauce (page 112), in your favorite lasagna, or even in brownies.

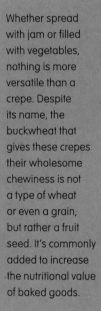

buckwheat crepes

Whether spread with jam or filled with vegetables, nothing is more versatile than a crepe. Despite its name, the buckwheat that gives these crepes their wholesome chewiness is not a type of wheat or even a grain, but rather a fruit seed. It's commonly added to increase the nutritional value of baked goods.

buckwheat flour, 2/3 cup

whole-wheat pastry flour, 1/3 cup

large eggs, 2

whole milk, 1 1/4 cups

honey, 1 Tbsp

salt, 1/4 tsp

unsalted butter for pan

MAKES 9 OR 10 CREPES

- In a medium bowl, combine flours, eggs, milk, honey, and salt and beat until combined. Batter will be thin and runny.

- Heat a lightly greased 10-inch crepe pan or frying pan over medium heat. Pour in 1/4 cup of batter and tilt pan to coat bottom evenly with a thin layer. Cook crepe until top is set and bottom is lightly browned, about 1 1/2 minutes. Using a heatproof rubber spatula and your fingers, loosen crepe around edges and flip. Cook until second side is browned, about 30 seconds. Repeat with remaining batter, brushing pan lightly with butter before cooking each crepe. Stack finished crepes between layers of waxed paper to prevent sticking.

- Crepes can be spread or filled with any ingredient you like.

Sweet and Savory Flavoring Suggestions

- Spread crepes with a layer of cream cheese and a layer of jam or applesauce. Roll up tightly and cut crosswise into rounds.

- Cut crepe into strips for dipping in Blueberry Sauce (page 38) and/or yogurt.

- After flipping, while the crepe is still in the pan, sprinkle with grated Parmesan or Cheddar cheese and let melt. Cut cooled crepe into bite-sized pieces.

- Spread crepes with Asparagus Puree (page 33) and ricotta cheese, cut into 4 wedges, and fold into triangles.

To store Wrap the wax paper–layered crepes and refrigerate for up to 3 days or freeze for up to 3 months.

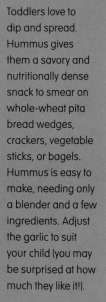

toddler's hummus

Toddlers love to dip and spread. Hummus gives them a savory and nutritionally dense snack to smear on whole-wheat pita bread wedges, crackers, vegetable sticks, or bagels. Hummus is easy to make, needing only a blender and a few ingredients. Adjust the garlic to suit your child (you may be surprised at how much they like it!).

canned chick-peas, 2 cups

tahini sauce (sesame paste), 1/3 cup

garlic, 1 clove, minced (optional)

lemon, 1, juiced

extra-virgin olive oil, 2 Tbsp, or as needed

ground cumin, 1/2 tsp

MAKES 2 1/3 CUPS

● Rinse chickpeas until water runs clear, and drain thoroughly.

● Combine chickpeas, tahini, garlic (if using), 1 Tbsp lemon juice, 1 Tbsp of the oil, and cumin in a food processor or blender and process until smooth. Scrape down sides of bowl and add remaining 1 Tbsp oil. Process until pastelike, 20–30 seconds longer.

● Taste and adjust flavor and consistency with additional lemon juice or oil.

To store Refrigerate hummus in an airtight container for up to 1 week.

toasted pita wedges

pita bread rounds, 2

olive oil, 1 Tbsp

spice(s) of choice, 1/2 tsp (optional)

MAKES 16 WEDGES

● Preheat oven to 375°F. Cut each pita round into 8 wedges, like a pie. Brush wedges with olive oil and put on a baking sheet. Sprinkle with desired spice. Bake until crisp, about 10 minutes.

Notes Feel free to spice these wedges up any way you like, from cinnamon and brown sugar to garlic salt and cumin. To store, refrigerate in an airtight container for up to 4 days.

avocado dip

avocado, 1 large

**fresh lime juice,
1 Tbsp**

**fresh cilantro,
1 Tbsp minced**

**green onion,
1 tsp minced**

salt, ½ tsp

MAKES ¾ CUP

- Halve avocado and remove pit. Scoop flesh into a small mixing bowl and mash with a fork.

- Add lime juice, cilantro, green onion, and salt and stir to combine.

To store Wrap with plastic wrap, pressing wrap against surface of the dip to slow discoloration, and refrigerate for up to 2 days.

Avocados often remain a favorite food throughout toddler- and childhood, making a filling snack that's rich in brain-building fats. Here is baby's first introduction to guacamole—hold the chiles. Increase the amount of onion for babies who enjoy the flavor or for grown-ups who are sharing. Serve with fun-shaped chips made from plain, flavored, or whole-wheat flour tortillas, vegetable strips, or pita wedges (opposite).

tortilla chips

olive-oil spray

**9-inch flour
tortillas, 5**

MAKES ABOUT
20 CHIPS

- Preheat oven to 375°F. Line a baking sheet with aluminum foil and spray with oil.

- Using 2- to 3-inch cookie cutters, cut tortillas into desired shapes. Place tortilla shapes in a single layer on prepared baking sheet. Spray shapes lightly with oil and bake until crisp, 5–7 minutes.

Notes For younger babies who are not ready for crunchy chips, simply cut out shapes and serve them untoasted. The longer these cook, the crisper they will become. The scraps created by cutting out shapes can also be toasted or eaten plain. Kids enjoy the funny little shapes.

pumpkin soup with alphabet pasta

butter, 1 Tbsp

onion, 1 Tbsp finely diced

Winter Squash Puree made with pumpkin (page 24) or canned pumpkin puree, 1 cup

low-sodium chicken broth, 2 cups

Apple Puree (page 27) or applesauce, 1 Tbsp

allspice, 1/8 tsp

dried thyme, 1/8 tsp

alphabet noodles, 1/4 cup

MAKES 2 1/2 CUPS

- In a medium saucepan over medium heat, melt butter. Add onion and cook until fragrant, about 30 seconds.

- Add pumpkin puree, broth, apple puree, allspice, and thyme and bring to a boil.

- Add alphabet noodles and cook just until tender, 8–10 minutes, or according to package directions. Let cool slightly before serving.

To store Refrigerate soup in an airtight container for up to 3 days.

What a fun way to learn the alphabet. If you still have pumpkin or other winter squash puree on hand in the freezer from baby's younger days, use that. Or, use canned, which in addition to being convenient can offer even more beta-carotene and vitamin A than fresh puree because of its low water content You'll find plain and vegetable flavored alphabet noodles at specialty grocers, or try other tiny pasta shapes, such as little rings (anelli) or stars (stelline).

minty eggplant dip

**eggplant,
1 medium**

**plain whole-milk
Greek yogurt,
1 cup**

**fresh mint,
2 Tbsp chopped**

raw sugar, 1 tsp

**fresh lime juice,
2 Tbsp**

**Toasted Pita
Wedges
(page 98) for
serving**

MAKES ABOUT
2 CUPS

● Preheat oven to 375°F. Line a baking dish with aluminum foil.

● Slice off and discard stalk end of eggplant and place eggplant in prepared baking dish. Roast until eggplant is very tender when pierced with the tip of a knife and flesh is soft enough to scoop, 45–50 minutes. When cool enough to handle, peel away skin and coarsely chop flesh. Puree eggplant in a food processor until smooth. You will have about 1 cup puree.

● In a large bowl, whisk yogurt until smooth and add eggplant puree, mint, sugar, and lime juice. Serve dip with pita wedges.

Notes If thick Greek yogurt is unavailable, substitute plain whole-milk yogurt. Use the creamy top layer, if possible, since this part will be thick like Greek yogurt. A thinner yogurt consistency will work just as well for dipping. To store, refrigerate dip in an airtight container for up to 3 days.

If your child balks at eggplant, it might help to let him know it's a fruit, not a vegetable, and that its French name, aubergine, is also used to describe its lovely purple color. It's greatly enjoyed all over the world, from China to the Mediterranean. This refreshing Indian-inspired dip blends eggplant with yogurt, mint, and a touch of sugar.

turkey minestrone

leek, ½

carrot, 1, peeled

zucchini, 1

green beans, 1 handful

celery rib, 1

tomatoes, 3 medium

canned cannellini beans, 1 cup

olive oil, 3 Tbsp

ground turkey, ½ lb

salt and pepper

dried oregano, 1 tsp

low-sodium vegetable broth, 1 qt (4 cups)

tomato paste, 2 Tbsp

fresh thyme leaves, 1 Tbsp

elbow macaroni, ¼ cup

MAKES ABOUT 6 CUPS

- Thinly slice leek. Chop carrot, zucchini, green beans, celery, and tomatoes. Set aside. Rinse beans until water runs clear and drain thoroughly. Set aside.

- In a large saucepan over medium heat, heat oil. Add turkey, season with salt and pepper, and sprinkle with oregano. Cook, stirring to break up turkey meat, until turkey is no longer pink, 4–5 minutes. Remove turkey with a slotted spoon and set aside. Add leek, carrot, zucchini, green beans, and celery to pan. Cover, reduce heat to low, and cook, stirring occasionally, for 15 minutes.

- Stir in broth, tomatoes, tomato paste, and thyme and increase heat to medium-high. Bring to a boil, cover, reduce heat to low, and simmer gently for 20 minutes.

- Add cannellini beans and macaroni and simmer until pasta is al dente, about 10 minutes, or according to package directions. Stir in turkey and cook to heat through, about 5 minutes. Season to taste with salt and pepper and serve.

To store Refrigerate soup in an airtight container for up to 5 days.

Minestrone soup is a great way to use an abundance of fresh produce and herbs from your garden or the farmers' market— and also to give the whole family a delicious dose of vegetables with a wide array of vitamins. Feel free to substitute leftover meats in place of the turkey, or to skip the meat and serve with crusty bread for a classic vegetarian meal. The beans will provide protein.

corn & salmon chowder

This dish is perfect for a weekend family supper. Since many kids are like Goldilocks and don't like foods that are either too hot or too cold, you may need to serve your child's soup at room temperature. Make sure to cut up larger chunks in baby's portion as needed; corn kernels in particular can be a hazard to those still learning to chew.

red potatoes,
½ lb

onion, ¼ cup
diced

celery rib, 1

carrot, 1 medium,
peeled

garlic, 1 clove

olive oil, 1 Tbsp

bay leaf, 1

low-sodium
vegetable broth,
1½ cups

skinless salmon
fillet, ¾ lb

whole milk,
1½ cups

corn kernels,
fresh or frozen,
1½ cups

salt and pepper

MAKES ABOUT
6 CUPS

● Peel and dice potatoes and set aside. Dice onion, celery, and carrot. Mince garlic.

● In a soup pot over medium heat, heat oil. Add onion, celery, carrot, garlic, and bay leaf and sauté until vegetables turn golden, 5–7 minutes. Reduce heat to medium-low, cover, and cook, stirring occasionally, until vegetables are tender, about 10 minutes. Add broth and potatoes, increase heat to high, and bring to a boil. Reduce heat to medium-low, cover, and simmer until potatoes are tender, about 12 minutes.

● Cut salmon into 1-inch pieces.

● Puree milk and 1 cup corn in a blender. Add corn puree, ½ cup corn kernels, and salmon pieces to pot. Return to medium heat and simmer, uncovered, until salmon is cooked through and soup is hot, 5–7 minutes. Discard bay leaf. Season to taste with salt and pepper.

● If soup is too chunky for your toddler, pass her portion through a food mill or pulse in a food processor.

Notes Salmon is a good fish for children, low in mercury but offering plenty of the omega-3 fats that help brain development and heart health. However, if allergies run in your family, you may wish to delay introducing fish; consult your pediatrician. To store, refrigerate chowder in an airtight container for up to 2 days.

12 to 18 months

lentil burgers with mint-yogurt sauce

The mint sauce gives these lentil burgers a bright boost of moisture and flavor. Lentils are available in a rainbow of colors: green, brown, red, yellow, and black. This vegetarian burger uses meaty brown lentils, rich in protein, fiber, minerals, and the B vitamins, especially folate.

brown lentils, 3/4 cup, picked over and rinsed

old-fashioned rolled oats, 1/2 cup

garlic, 1 clove, minced

ground cumin, 1 tsp

mild curry powder, 1 tsp

large egg, 1, beaten

salt and freshly ground pepper

plain whole-milk yogurt, 1 cup

fresh mint, 2/3 cup minced

canola oil, 1 Tbsp

MAKES SIX 4-INCH BURGERS

• In a large saucepan over medium-high heat, combine 2 cups water and lentils. Bring to a boil, cover, and simmer until lentils are tender, about 15 minutes. Drain.

• Meanwhile, in a food processor, grind oats to a coarse meal.

• In a large bowl, mash lentils with a potato masher or a fork. Add 3 Tbsp ground oats, garlic, cumin, and curry powder and mix together. Add egg and season with salt and pepper. Using your hands, form mixture into six 4-inch patties, each 1/2 inch thick. Coat patties in remaining oats and chill them, uncovered, in the refrigerator for 10 minutes.

• In a small bowl, stir together yogurt and mint to make a sauce. Set aside.

• In a large frying pan over medium-high heat, heat oil. Fry burgers, turning once, until brown and crisp, 3–4 minutes per side.

• Depending on your toddler's age and chewing ability, spread burgers with sauce and cut into small pieces, or cut burgers into strips for dipping in sauce.

Notes For older children and adults, serve the burgers in split pita bread rounds, with butter lettuce leaves, tomato slices, and a dollop of mint-yogurt sauce. To store, refrigerate burgers in an airtight container for up to 2 days, or wrap in waxed paper, seal in freezer bags, and freeze for up to 1 month. Refrigerate sauce for up to 3 days.

12 to 18 months

little vegetable fritters

sweet potato, 1 medium

zucchini, 1 large

corn flour, 1 cup

baking powder, ½ tsp

salt and pepper

egg, 1, beaten

canola oil, 2 Tbsp

whole milk, ¼ cup

sour cream or mustard for dipping

MAKES 15 TWO-INCH FRITTERS

- Preheat oven to 250°F.

- Peel and grate sweet potato. Grate zucchini, leaving skin on. You will have about 1 cup of each. Wrap grated vegetables in a clean kitchen towel or paper towels and gently squeeze to extract as much liquid as possible. Transfer to a medium mixing bowl.

- In a small bowl, combine corn flour and baking powder. Season with salt and pepper. Add flour mixture and egg to vegetables and stir just until combined.

- In a large frying pan over medium heat, heat oil. Scoop out large tablespoonfuls of batter, form into rounded balls with wet hands, and flatten into cakes. In batches, cook cakes, turning once, until brown and crisp, 2–3 minutes total. Using a slotted spoon and letting the oil drip back into the pan, transfer to paper towels to drain, then place on a baking sheet in a low oven to keep warm until all fritters are made. Repeat with remaining vegetable mixture.

- Serve with a small bowl of sour cream or, for adventurous little eaters, mustard, for dipping.

Some babies eat so much pureed yam and other beta carotene–rich foods in their first few months of eating solids that their skin turns a little orange, and their parents would be happy never to see another sweet potato. Here's a radically different way to feed your youngster this nutritional power house. Crisp on the outside and moist on the inside, this preparation will induce even the choosiest toddler to not only eat, but enjoy, his veggies.

tempting a toddler

Toddlerhood is a time of rapid changes. Your child may start to reject formerly favored foods, become obsessed with a particular food for a week, or eat so little you worry for her health. Understanding the reasons behind the changes may help you stay relaxed about altered eating habits.

Picky eating may be a self-protective instinct in young children. Many vegetables have a bitter flavor, and in nature bitterness can indicate a poisonous plant. While a poisonous plant might do no more than make an adult ill, it might kill a child. Some scientists believe that this is the reason children seem designed to play it safe when it comes to food. Other reasons for changes in eating habits follow.

Slower grower   Your child's growth has slowed considerably after the first year. A toddler does not need as much food, relatively, as a baby.

Busy bee   Your toddler is too busy and bursting with energy to sit still for lengthy meals. Eating several small meals throughout the day is a more natural pattern for children in this age group than 3 big meals (and may be a healthier way for adults to eat, as well).

Free will   Toddlers are learning to exercise their will, and mealtimes can become a focal point. Let your child make the decision of what and how much to eat by simply offering a variety of healthy foods at each meal.

Refined palate   Children's taste buds are sharper and more numerous than adults', so their food simply tastes stronger to them. As noted above, bitter foods, such as many vegetables, are particularly bothersome. To camouflage them, blend with other foods.

Seeks comfort   Toddlers are exploring an ever-widening world, but they desire to balance novelty with familiarity and predictability, especially at mealtime and bedtime. It may take as many as 15 tries before a new food becomes familiar and is accepted.

Short circuit   Toddlers are easily overwhelmed. If you put a large quantity of food on your child's highchair tray, it may look to him like too much to eat, and end up as a plaything or on the floor. Serve her food to her a little at a time.

making food fun

Try to understand your little one's changing food needs to avoid mealtime battles. A frustrated attitude or annoyed expression from you may only entertain your child, or cause unnecessary stress. Although you cannot force a child to eat, and pressuring or even coaxing a reluctant eater is questionable, you can make foods more appealing and fun to entice your toddler to linger at the table.

In order to foster a healthy attitude toward food in your child, avoid using certain foods (such as sweets) as a reward or treat. The best tactic is to keep the mood at the table upbeat and to let your child see you eating and enjoying all the good foods you're serving to him.

Dip right in Give your toddler fruit slices, vegetable sticks, and toast pieces to dip into healthy dips made with yogurt, beans, cream cheese, avocado, and fruit or vegetable purees.

Spread it on Toddlers like spreading, smearing, and painting activities. Give them their own small cheese spreader or pastry brush to smear soft cheese, vegetable puree, and fruit concentrate onto crackers, toast, or rice cakes.

Top it Letting toddlers add a familiar flavor, texture, or color to the top of new and less-desirable foods is a way to broaden the choosy toddler's menu. Favorite toppings include grated cheese, guacamole, tomato sauce, applesauce, and granola.

Drink up If your youngster would rather drink than eat, create a healthy smoothie using milk, fresh fruit, juice, wheat germ, yogurt, and honey (after 1 year). Or, make cold soups from fresh vegetables, yogurt, broths, and herbs. These can be enjoyed from a cup or bowl or through a straw.

Decorate it Think of creative ways to present foods: sandwiches cut into stars, pancakes with berry faces. Arm yourself with cookie cutters, squeeze bottles, and your imagination.

Do it together Even very little kids like to help. Let them help wash vegetables or mix cut-up fruits in a bowl to make a salad, and they'll be more interested in eating their own handiwork. Bring them to the market to help pick out the good foods they'll eat later, too.

orzo with rainbow vegetables

salt

orzo, ½ cup

extra-virgin olive
oil, 1 Tbsp

fresh rosemary,
1 tsp minced

red and yellow
bell pepper,
½ cup diced

fresh or frozen
peas, ½ cup

fresh lemon juice,
1 tsp

pepper, ⅛ tsp

MAKES 2 CUPS

● Bring a pot of water to a boil. Add a large pinch of salt and the orzo. Cook, stirring occasionally, until just tender, about 10 minutes, or according to package directions. Drain.

● In a frying pan over medium heat, heat oil. Add rosemary and sauté until aromatic, about 30 seconds. Add bell peppers and peas and sauté until tender, about 3 minutes.

● Add orzo to pan and toss with vegetables. Sprinkle with lemon juice and season with salt and pepper.

To store Refrigerate orzo in an airtight container for up to 3 days.

This colorful dish can be made easily with any of your family's favorite vegetables in place of the peas and peppers, such as squash, corn, or carrots. Each different color of vegetable offers a different set of disease-fighting antioxidants, so choose as wide a range of hues as possible when preparing this dish. Although orzo looks like a grain, it is actually small barley-shaped pasta.

hidden veggie sauce

Sometimes parents need to be sly to get children to eat vegetables. This sauce contains 2 secret vitamin-packed ingredients that you don't have to reveal to your offspring: spinach and yams. The thick and hearty red sauce can be used to top pasta or Meatballs with Polenta (page 114), or it can be served as a dip.

olive oil, 2 Tbsp

onion, 1/2, finely diced

garlic, 1 clove, minced

Pureed Spinach, (page 95), 1/4 cup

Sweet Potato Puree (page 26), 1/4 cup

tomato paste, 1 Tbsp

dried oregano, 1/4 tsp

pepper, 1/4 tsp

strained tomatoes, one 26-ounce carton

blackstrap molasses (see Notes), 1 Tbsp

ricotta cheese, 1/3 cup

MAKES 4 CUPS

● In a large saucepan over medium heat, heat oil. Add onion and cook, stirring occasionally, until translucent, about 4 minutes. Add garlic and cook until aromatic, about 1 minute. Reduce heat to low, add spinach and sweet potato purees, tomato paste, oregano, and pepper and cook, stirring frequently, for 4 minutes. Increase heat to high, add tomatoes and molasses, and bring to a boil. Reduce heat to low and simmer uncovered, stirring occasionally, for 20 minutes.

● Divide sauce in half and refrigerate or freeze 1 portion for a later use. Serve sauce over pasta or on the side, for little dippers. Top each serving with a small dollop of ricotta cheese.

Notes Regular molasses can be used, but blackstrap molasses will add extra iron to this dish, and the vitamin C in the tomatoes will help the body absorb the iron. To store, refrigerate sauce in an airtight container for up to 4 days, or freeze for up to 3 months.

12 to 18 months

aromatic couscous

golden raisins,
1/4 cup

unsalted butter,
1 Tbsp

salt, 1/2 tsp

ground cinnamon
and cumin,
1/4 tsp each

Israeli couscous,
1 cup

MAKES ABOUT
4 CUPS

● In a saucepan over medium-high heat, combine 1¼ cups water, raisins, butter, salt, cinnamon, and cumin and bring to a boil. Stir in couscous, reduce heat to low, and simmer for 3 minutes. Remove from heat, cover, and let stand 5 minutes. Give a final stir and serve.

Notes Regular couscous, prepared according to the package directions, may be substituted for Israeli couscous—but the results will be less rich and creamy. If desired, stir in 1 cup cut-up Lemon-Mint Chicken (below) just after removing from heat. To store, refrigerate couscous in an airtight container for up to 3 days.

lemon-mint chicken

olive oil, 1 tsp

fresh lemon juice,
1 Tbsp

fresh mint,
1 tsp minced

salt and pepper

skinless, boneless
chicken breast,
1 (about 9 oz)

MAKES ONE 9-OZ
CHICKEN BREAST

● Preheat oven to 400°F. Set an oiled rack in an aluminum foil–lined baking pan.

● In a small bowl, whisk together oil, lemon juice, mint, and salt and pepper to taste.

● Put chicken on prepared rack and drizzle with oil and lemon mixture. Bake, turning once, until chicken is cooked through and no longer pink in the center, 12–15 minutes per side.

To store Refrigerate in an airtight container for up to 3 days.

The use of cinnamon in a savory dish is typical of Middle Eastern cuisine, and if you add chicken, you'll find that this warm spice will complement it unexpectedly well. Couscous is not a grain, as many people assume, but rather little balls of pasta made from semolina wheat. Israeli couscous is white and larger than the more common Mediterranean variety, and can be found in the dry bulk sections of specialty grocers.

meatballs with polenta

Here is the original Italian comfort food! Oat bran takes the place of the traditional bread crumbs in these meatballs for added moisture and nutrition. Next time, serve the meatballs with mashed potatoes and lingonberry preserves for a Swedish variation on classic meatballs with tomato sauce.

olive-oil spray

oat bran, ½ cup

whole milk, ¼ cup

ground beef, 1 lb

garlic, 1 clove, minced or grated

dried dill, 1 Tbsp

nutmeg, ⅛ tsp freshly grated

salt, ¼ tsp

pepper, ¼ tsp

egg, 1, lightly beaten

Polenta (page 94), for serving

Hidden Veggie Sauce (page 112), for serving

MAKES 45–50 MINI MEATBALLS

● Preheat oven to 400°F. Line 2 baking sheets with aluminum foil and spray with oil.

● In a large bowl, combine oat bran and milk. Add beef, garlic, dill, nutmeg, salt, pepper, and egg. Using your hands, combine ingredients just until blended. Be careful not to overwork. Scoop up rounded teaspoonfuls of beef mixture, roll into mini meatballs, and set on prepared baking sheets.

● Bake until browned and cooked through, 10–12 minutes.

● Spoon meatballs over polenta and top with sauce.

Notes Feel free to use fennel seeds, oregano, or any of your family's favorite herbs and spices in place of the nutmeg and dill, for variety. To store, refrigerate meatballs in an airtight container for up to 3 days, or freeze up to 3 months. If you like, garnish with a dollop of ricotta cheese.

salmon cakes

These little cornmeal cakes are a good way to get beneficial fish into a picky eater's diet. In fact, mild-tasting polenta makes a great vehicle for just about any meat, vegetable, spice, or sauce. Baking and cutting the polenta allows little fingers to pick it up easily. Fresh lemon juice gives these cakes a bright flavor that goes well with fish.

low-sodium vegetable broth, 2 cups

dried dill, 1 tsp

salt, 1/8 tsp

pepper, 1/8 tsp

fresh lemon juice, 1 tsp

skinless salmon fillet, 1/4 lb, cut into 2-inch chunks

instant polenta, 3/4 cup

unsalted butter, 1 tsp

MAKES NINE 2½-INCH-SQUARE CAKES

● Preheat oven to 400°F. Line an 8-inch-square glass baking dish with parchment paper or aluminum foil, allowing some overhang over sides of dish.

● In a medium saucepan over medium heat, bring 2 cups water, broth, dill, salt, pepper, and lemon juice to a boil. Add salmon and simmer until pieces are opaque, 4–5 minutes. Remove salmon chunks with a slotted spoon, reserving cooking liquid, and put in a shallow bowl. Using a fork, flake salmon into small pieces.

● Return cooking liquid to a simmer and slowly whisk in polenta. Reduce heat to low and cook, stirring frequently to prevent sticking and bubbling, until polenta has absorbed all of the liquid and thickened, about 10 minutes. Be cautious, as polenta will bubble, pop, and spit if heat is too high. Remove from heat and stir in butter and flaked salmon.

● Pour polenta into prepared dish and bake until set and golden on top, 30–35 minutes. Remove dish from oven and let stand for 10–15 minutes to firm. Lift parchment to transfer polenta to a plate, and slice into squares or pieces, as small or large as your toddler can handle.

Notes If allergies run in your family, you may wish to delay introducing fish; consult your pediatrician. To store, refrigerate salmon cakes in an airtight container for 1 or 2 days.

12 to 18 months

tabbouleh

bulgur wheat,
½ cup

boiling water,
1 cup

fresh lemon juice,
¼ cup

fresh mint,
⅓ cup minced

olive oil, ¼ cup

salt and pepper

fresh flat-leaf
parsley,
1 large bunch

tomato,
1 medium

green onion, 1

Lemon-Mint
Chicken (page
113), shredded

MAKES ABOUT
2 CUPS

- Put bulgur in a large glass bowl and pour boiling water over it. Let sit at room temperature for 1 hour. Most of the water will be absorbed. Drain, squeezing remaining water out of bulgur with your hands.

- In a small bowl, whisk together lemon juice, mint, and oil. Season with salt and pepper. Pour dressing over bulgur wheat and mix until grains are coated.

- Remove stems from parsley and discard. Mince leaves in food processor and measure out 1 cup. Dice tomato and green onion. Add parsley, tomato, and green onion to bulgur mixture, and stir.

- Cover and refrigerate for 1 hour or up to 1 day for grain to absorb dressing and flavors to blend. Fluff with a fork before serving.

Notes You can find bulgur in the pasta and rice aisle or in the dry bulk bins of the grocery store. To store, refrigerate salad in an airtight container for up to 3 days.

Bright green parsley, bursting with antioxidants, healthy and savory olive oil, and fiber-rich whole-grain bulgur wheat combine to make a very healthful dish, a classic in the Lebanese kitchen. Because the bulgur needs time to soak both before and after it is seasoned, advance preparation is necessary. But the flavor and texture are so good that this dish is guaranteed to become a family favorite.

chicken & mango quesadillas

8-inch whole-wheat tortillas, 4

vegetable oil

Cheddar cheese, 1½ cups grated

shredded Lemon-Mint Chicken (page 113), 1½ cups

mango, 1, peeled, pitted, and sliced

fresh cilantro, ¼ cup chopped

prepared mild salsa and/or sour cream for serving (optional)

MAKES
2 QUESADILLAS

● Preheat oven to 375°F. Brush 2 tortillas with oil. Place tortillas, oil side down, on a baking sheet. Sprinkle each with one-quarter of the cheese, half of the chicken, half of the mango, half of the cilantro, and another one-quarter of the cheese. Top each with 1 tortilla, pressing to adhere; brush top with oil.

● Bake quesadillas until filling is heated through and edges begin to crisp, about 10 minutes. Using a large metal spatula, carefully turn each over and bake until bottom is crisp, about 5 minutes.

● Transfer quesadillas to plates. Using a pizza cutter, cut into wedges as wide or narrow as your toddler can handle. Let cheese cool sufficiently to prevent burning little tongues before serving with mild salsa and/or sour cream, if desired.

To store Wrap cooled quesadillas well in plastic wrap and refrigerate for up to 3 days, or freeze for up to 2 weeks.

Mangoes, so rich in vitamins A and C, give the everyday quesadilla a tropical flair. These quesadillas are a great way to make a second meal out of leftover chicken, beef, or pork. The cheese adds additional protein for growing kids, and the tortillas offer carbs for energy. You can change the color and flavor of these quesadillas by choosing from a variety of flavored tortillas: spinach, corn, and tomato are a few of the options available.

toddler's burrito

The burrito truly is the beast of burden of the food world, dutifully carrying any ingredients you care to heap on. The sticky mashed beans keep the good stuff from falling out during eating, and pairing them with chewy brown rice makes a complete protein. Warm the beans just enough to melt the cheese when it's all wrapped up.

pinto beans, one 15-oz can

Toddler's Brown Rice, 3/4 cup (page 62)

sharp Cheddar cheese, 3/4 cup grated

prepared mild salsa, 2–3 Tbsp (optional)

8-inch whole-wheat tortillas, 6

MAKES SIX 6-BY-2-INCH BURRITOS

● Rinse beans until water runs clear and drain thoroughly. Transfer to a large bowl and mash with a potato masher. In a saucepan over medium heat, warm the beans.

● Add rice, cheese, and salsa (if using) to beans and mix until blended. Divide mixture evenly among tortillas. Fold in 2 ends and roll burritos.

To store Perfect for little hands, burritos can be kept in the freezer for a last-minute lunch or dinner or for a take-along meal. Wrap burritos individually in aluminum foil, seal in a large freezer bag, and freeze for up to 3 months. To thaw frozen burrito, place in refrigerator overnight.

vegetable oven fries

extra-virgin olive oil

beets, 1/2 lb

rutabaga, 1 (1/2 lb)

sweet potato, 1 (1/2 lb)

fresh thyme, 1 Tbsp minced

fresh flat-leaf parsley, 1 Tbsp minced

fresh sage, 1 Tbsp minced

sea salt, 1/2 tsp

MAKES ABOUT 2 CUPS

- Preheat oven to 500°F. Line 2 baking sheets with aluminum foil and oil foil.

- Peel beets, rutabaga, and sweet potatoes. With a sharp knife or mandoline, cut each root into slices 1/2 inch thick, then cut slices into strips 1/2 inch wide.

- In a small bowl, mix thyme, parsley, sage, and salt. In a large bowl, toss vegetables with 2 Tbsp oil and mixed herbs.

- Spread vegetables in a single layer on prepared baking sheets. Bake, turning occasionally with tongs, until vegetables are tender and golden, 20–25 minutes. Transfer to a platter and blot with paper towels.

- Cut strips into dice as needed, as small or large as your toddler can handle.

Notes Beets will stain other vegetables, fingertips, and clothing pink. If you want to keep the rutabaga white, separate beets and season them in their own bowl. To store, refrigerate vegetable fries in an airtight container for up to 3 days.

These easy oven fries, made from a mix of red beets, white rutabaga, and orange sweet potatoes, are not only colorful and delicious, but are also chock-full of beta-carotene and a range of vitamins and minerals. Made with olive oil and not truly fried, they are guilt-free for grown-ups. The added sprinkling of fresh herbs makes them appealing to children and adults alike. Feel free to use a single favorite root vegetable instead of a mix.

mac & cheese

elbow macaroni,
½ lb

broccoli and/or
cauliflower,
1½ cups small,
equal-sized
florets

whole milk, 1 cup

sharp white
Cheddar cheese,
¾ lb shredded
(about 3 cups)

salt

pepper, ¼ tsp

Parmesan
cheese, 3 Tbsp
grated

MAKES ABOUT
4 CUPS

● Preheat oven to 350°F. Bring a pot of water to a boil over high heat. Reduce heat to medium and add macaroni and vegetables. Simmer until macaroni is al dente and vegetables are tender but not mushy, 7–10 minutes. Drain pasta and vegetables and return them to pot.

● Heat milk in a small saucepan over low heat. Add hot milk and Cheddar cheese to macaroni and vegetables, and toss to combine. Season with salt to taste and pepper, and stir again.

● Pour pasta mixture into an 8-inch-square glass or ceramic baking dish. Sprinkle Parmesan cheese over top. Bake until bubbling, about 15 minutes. Allow to sit for 5–10 minutes before serving.

To store Refrigerate for up to 3 days or freeze for up to 2 months.

Even the boxed brands of macaroni and cheese on the supermarket shelves have to be cooked, so making this favorite casserole from scratch doesn't add much effort— and the results are dramatically better. Make it with or without vegetables. Broccoli and cauliflower pieces are a convenient choice because their cooking time is the same as for the pasta.

little dippers fish fingers

This baked fish dish works well with meaty mahimahi, but you can use any firm white fish. Fish is a great source of protein and heart-healthy omega-3 fats, and lean white fish is milder in flavor than oily fish like salmon, making it a good choice for fussy eaters. The bright flavor of dill pairs well with fish, but use any herb you like. *Panko*, Japanese bread crumbs, are lighter and crunchier than ordinary crumbs.

vegetable-oil spray

mahimahi fillets, 1 lb

whole milk, 1/4 cup

unbleached flour, 1/4 cup

panko **or regular bread crumbs, 2/3 cup**

fresh dill, 1 tsp minced, or dried dill, 1/2 tsp

pepper, 1/8 tsp

unsalted butter, 2 Tbsp melted

lemon or lime wedges for serving

yogurt for serving

MAKES ABOUT 8 FISH FINGERS

● Preheat oven to 450°F. Line 2 baking sheets with aluminum foil and spray with oil.

● Rinse fish and pat dry with a paper towel. Cut into serving-sized pieces (1 1/2–2 inches across), and measure thickness of fillets to determine cooking time.

● Put milk in a shallow bowl. Put flour on a plate. In another shallow bowl, combine *panko*, dill, pepper, and melted butter.

● Dip each piece of fish in milk, then coat with flour. Dip again in milk and roll in *panko* mixture. Place fish on prepared baking sheet. Bake until fish flakes easily, 4–6 minutes per 1/2 inch of thickness.

● Serve with lemon or lime wedges and/or a dipping sauce made of yogurt blended with lime juice.

Notes In addition to the flavored yogurt, you can serve any dipping sauce your family enjoys: tartar sauce, cocktail sauce, and honey-mustard sauce are all delicious options. If allergies run in your family, you may wish to delay introducing fish; consult your pediatrician. To store, refrigerate in an airtight container for up to 2 days.

hearty
beef stew

creamer potatoes, 3 medium

beef tenderloin, 1 lb

olive oil, 2 tsp

salt and pepper

garlic, 1 clove, minced

fresh rosemary, 1 Tbsp minced

pearl onions, 15, peeled (see Notes)

carrots, 2 medium, peeled and cut into 1-inch rounds

low-sodium vegetable broth, 1½ cups

balsamic vinegar, 2 Tbsp

plain whole-milk yogurt, 1 Tbsp

MAKES ABOUT 4 CUPS

● Cut potatoes into 1-inch cubes and set aside. Trim excess fat from beef and cut into 1-inch cubes.

● In a large sauté pan over high heat, heat oil. Season beef with salt and pepper and cook, turning once, until browned, about 3 minutes. Transfer to a plate.

● Add garlic and rosemary to pan and cook until fragrant, about 1 minute. Add onions, potatoes, carrots, broth, and vinegar; cover and bring to a boil. Reduce heat to medium and simmer until vegetables are tender, 40–45 minutes. Return beef to pan and simmer until heated through, about 5 minutes. Stir in yogurt to thicken sauce.

● Depending on your toddler's age and chewing ability, shred beef in his portion.

Notes To peel pearl onions, drop whole onions into boiling water for 3 minutes. Scoop out and immerse in cold water to stop the cooking. Cut off root ends and gently squeeze opposite end to remove skin. You can also buy the onions already peeled, in jars or frozen. To store, refrigerate stew in an airtight container for up to 3 days, or freeze for up to 3 months.

This is a hearty protein- and iron-rich winter night's dish for the whole family. Tiny pearl onions are especially appealing to kids. The meat and vegetables will be quite tender after long simmering, but your toddler's portion may be cut up further as needed. A younger baby's serving can be partially pureed if she is not yet ready for a coarse texture. This dish is good spooned over whole grains and pasta, such as brown rice, polenta, quinoa, or couscous.

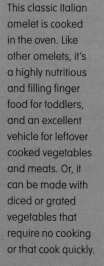

frittata

This classic Italian omelet is cooked in the oven. Like other omelets, it's a highly nutritious and filling finger food for toddlers, and an excellent vehicle for leftover cooked vegetables and meats. Or, it can be made with diced or grated vegetables that require no cooking or that cook quickly.

large eggs, 6

fresh herb of choice, 1 tsp minced

salt, 1/8 tsp

pepper, 1/8 tsp

unsalted butter, 1 Tbsp

onion, 1/4 cup finely diced

vegetables and/or meat of choice, 3/4 cup diced or grated, precooked or quick-cooking (see suggestions; optional)

cheese of choice, 1/3 cup crumbled or grated

MAKES ONE
10-INCH FRITTATA

- Preheat oven to 350°F. In a medium mixing bowl, whisk together eggs, herb, salt, pepper, and 1 Tbsp water.

- In a large ovenproof frying pan over medium heat, melt butter. Add onion and sauté until soft and translucent, about 3 minutes. Add vegetables and meat, if using, and sauté for 2 minutes to warm through. Shake pan to spread vegetables and/or meat evenly in pan. Remove pan from heat and pour in egg mixture. Sprinkle cheese over top.

- Bake frittata until center is set and cooked and edges are browned and pulling away from pan sides, 10–15 minutes. Remove from oven and let stand for 5 minutes. Cut into wedges or squares with a knife or pizza cutter.

Flavoring suggestions

Use cooked diced potatoes and ham, grated Gruyère cheese, and minced fresh rosemary.

Use grated or finely diced uncooked vegetables of choice (zucchini, red bell pepper, tomatoes), crumbled fresh goat cheese, and fresh basil or thyme. Or, use cooked diced vegetables.

Use chopped black Niçoise olives and sun-dried tomatoes, crumbled feta cheese, and fresh dill.

Notes If allergies run in your family, you may wish to delay introducing eggs; consult your pediatrician. To store, wrap frittata well and refrigerate for up to 1 day.

cranberry-orange scones

Your child may be interested to know that cranberries are also known as bounceberries because they do just that when ripe. Related to blueberries, they are one of the most antioxidant-rich fruits of all. These fruit-studded mini scones fit nicely into small hands at breakfast, brunch, or snack time.

whole-wheat pastry flour, 2½ cups

brown sugar, ½ cup firmly packed

baking powder, 2 tsp

baking soda, 1 tsp

salt, 1 tsp

orange zest, 1 Tbsp finely grated

unsalted butter, 6 Tbsp, cut into chunks

whole milk, ½ cup plus 1 Tbsp

large egg, 1, lightly beaten

fresh orange juice, 3 Tbsp

dried cranberries, ⅓ cup, chopped

MAKES 32 MINI SCONES

● Preheat oven to 400°F. Line 2 baking sheets with parchment paper or aluminum foil.

● In a food processor, combine flour, sugar, baking powder, baking soda, salt, and orange zest. Pulse to mix. Add butter and pulse until mixture resembles oatmeal. Add milk, egg, and orange juice and process until mixture comes together, about 20 seconds. Transfer dough to a bowl and stir in cranberries with a wooden spoon.

● Turn dough out onto a lightly floured work surface and lightly knead into a ball. Dough will be sticky and may need to be sprinkled with more flour. With a rolling pin, roll out dough ½ inch thick. Flour a 1½-inch round biscuit or cookie cutter and cut out as many scones as possible. Place on prepared baking sheets 2 inches apart. Gather scraps of dough, knead together, roll out, and cut out more scones. Repeat until dough is gone.

● Bake scones until golden, 6–7 minutes. With a spatula, transfer to a wire rack and let cool.

Notes Get creative by cutting these with shaped cookie cutters instead of rounds. If you have a child for your sous chef, be warned that this batter is very sticky and messy. To store, hold scones in an airtight container at room temperature for up to 3 days, or freeze for up to 3 months.

dried-apricot oatcakes

vegetable-oil spray

old-fashioned rolled oats, 2 cups

ground cinnamon, 1/2 tsp

baking soda, 1/2 tsp

salt, 1/8 tsp

unsalted butter, 2 Tbsp melted

honey, 1 Tbsp

dried apricots, 3 Tbsp finely chopped

finely shredded unsweetened coconut, 2 Tbsp

MAKES 15–18 TWO-INCH ROUNDS

● Preheat oven to 400°F. Line 2 baking sheets with aluminum foil and spray with oil.

● In a mixing bowl, combine oats, cinnamon, baking soda, and salt. Make a well in the center and add the butter and honey. Combine with a rubber spatula until all oats are coated. Mix in apricots and coconut. Heat 1 cup of water in a teakettle or saucepan until very hot but not boiling. Add hot water 2 tablespoonfuls at a time to oat mixture, stirring after each addition with a rubber spatula, until oats become wet and sticky. You will not need to use all of the water. With wet hands, mix oat dough a final time. Dough will be sticky and loose.

● Using 2 large spoons, scoop and drop dough onto prepared baking sheets. With wet fingertips, shape dough into 2-inch round, flat oatcakes.

● Bake oatcakes until edges turn golden brown and centers are firm and not sticky, about 15 minutes. Transfer to a wire rack to cool completely. The oatcakes will crisp while cooling.

To store Hold cakes in an airtight container at room temperature for up to 3 days, or freeze for up to 3 months.

Here's a way to feed your toddler his oatmeal without fighting over the spoon. You'll feel good about sharing this breakfast with your little one, as it provides all of the solid nutrition of whole-grain oats, plus a little fruit for good measure, without the sugars, additives, and preservatives found in most prepackaged breakfast bars.

weekend waffles

These light and fluffy waffles with a sweet banana-maple sauce are perfect for the whole family to make and eat together on the weekend. But think beyond Saturday and Sunday and make extra for your child to enjoy for a midweek breakfast or snack. In place of the banana sauce, try a simple topping of plain yogurt and fruit.

large eggs, 4, separated, at room temperature

fresh orange juice, 1/3 cup

vanilla extract, 1/2 tsp

whole milk, 1 1/4 cups

whole-wheat pastry flour, 1 cup

unbleached all-purpose flour, 1 cup

baking powder, 1 tsp

salt, 1/4 tsp

oil for greasing

banana, 1 large, sliced

pure maple syrup, 1/3 cup

MAKES 7 OR 8 EIGHT-INCH WAFFLES

● In a large bowl, gently whisk egg yolks to loosen. Add orange juice and vanilla and whisk to combine. Add milk and whisk gently just until combined.

● Put egg whites in a large, dry, clean mixing bowl. Using a handheld mixer on high speed, beat whites until stiff, glossy peaks form when the beater is lifted, about 2 minutes.

● In a large bowl, stir together flours, baking powder, and salt with a wooden spoon until blended. Slowly stir the dry ingredients into the egg yolk mixture and continue to stir until batter is smooth. Gently fold in egg whites with a rubber spatula just until combined.

● Preheat and grease a waffle iron. Pour enough batter over iron to fill it (about 3/4 cup), close, and let batter cook until signal indicates to open. Carefully remove waffle from iron and keep warm in a low (200°F) oven. Repeat with remaining batter.

● To make sauce: In a small saucepan over low heat, warm banana and syrup. Cook, stirring every few minutes with a heatproof spatula or wooden spoon to break up banana slices, until syrup is hot, 5–7 minutes.

● Serve waffles with hot banana-maple sauce. Some children at this stage like to dip. If your toddler does, cut waffle into strips and serve sauce alongside.

To store Refrigerate waffles in an airtight container for up to 3 days, or wrap in waxed paper, seal in freezer bags, and freeze for up to 1 month.

pumpkin pancakes

Pumpkin pancakes are a great autumn and winter weekend family tradition that can include toddlers, too. These flavorful pancakes offer a healthy dose of vitamins A and C and beta-carotene, thanks to the pumpkin. Serve with fresh fruit, plain yogurt, and/or pure maple syrup.

whole milk, 1 cup

canned pumpkin puree, 1/2 cup

large egg, 1, separated, at room temperature

canola oil, 2 Tbsp

white vinegar, 1 Tbsp

whole-wheat flour, 1 cup

brown sugar, 2 Tbsp

baking powder, 2 tsp

baking soda, 1 Tbsp

salt, 1 tsp

ground cinnamon, 1 tsp

ground allspice, 1/4 tsp

nutmeg, 1/4 tsp freshly grated

vegetable-oil spray

MAKES TEN 5-INCH PANCAKES

● In a large mixing bowl, whisk together milk, pumpkin, egg, oil, and vinegar until well blended.

● In a separate mixing bowl, stir together flour, sugar, baking powder, baking soda, salt, cinnamon, allspice, and nutmeg until blended. Stir flour mixture into pumpkin mixture with a wooden spoon just until blended. Let batter sit for 5 minutes for fluffier cakes. Batter will be thick.

● Spray a large nonstick griddle or frying pan with oil and heat over medium heat. Pour batter by 1/4 cupfuls into pan and spread with a spoon to flatten. Cook until bubbles form on top of pancakes, 2–3 minutes. Flip each pancake and cook until golden on second side, about 1 minute longer. Keep pancakes warm in a low oven. Repeat with remaining batter. Serve warm.

To store Refrigerate pancakes in an airtight container for up to 3 days, or wrap in waxed paper, seal in freezer bags, and freeze for up to 1 month.

rice pudding

kiwifruit, 1/3 cup
finely diced

mango, 1/3 cup
finely diced

papaya, 1/3 cup
finely diced

whole milk,
2 1/4 cups

basmati rice,
3/4 cup

vanilla extract,
1 tsp

nutmeg, 1/8 tsp
freshly grated

honey, 1/3 cup

evaporated milk,
1/3 cup

unsweetened
shredded dried
coconut, 1/3 cup

MAKES FOUR
3 1/2-INCH
RAMEKINS

- In a small bowl, combine kiwifruit, mango, and papaya, cover, and refrigerate until ready to use.

- In a large saucepan over medium heat, combine whole milk and rice and bring to a boil. Cover, reduce heat to low, and simmer until liquid is absorbed, about 15 minutes. Remove pan from heat. Stir in vanilla, nutmeg, honey, and evaporated milk. Add coconut and stir with a fork to break up rice and to combine all ingredients.

- Spoon mixture into four 3 1/2-inch ramekins and cover each with aluminum foil. Arrange ramekins in a baking pan, place on pulled-out oven rack, and pour warm water into pan to come about two-thirds of the way up the sides of the ramekins. Slide rack into oven and bake for 30 minutes. Remove foil and bake until top peaks of puddings are golden brown, 15 minutes longer. Remove from oven and let ramekins cool to the touch.

- Serve pudding in ramekins, topped with fruit, or slide a knife around edge of each ramekin and turn puddings over onto plates to serve with fruit on side or spooned over the tops.

Notes Feel free to substitute jasmine rice for a slightly sweeter flavor. To store, refrigerate puddings in an airtight container for up to 1 day.

This pudding, crowned with juicy, vitamin-rich tropical fruits, makes a special treat for little ones and a sweet ending to an adult meal. It's also an eggless version of this classic comfort food, good for babies and toddlers still eschewing eggs. Grown-ups can enjoy rice pudding hot, warm, or cold, but be sure to let baby's ramekin cool completely before bringing it to her.

carrot cupcakes

The perfect choice for celebrating baby's first birthday! These cupcakes have no chokable raisins or allergenic nuts for little revelers. Thanks to the carrots, they're wholesome as well as sweet and delicious. The versatile batter can easily be baked in either standard or miniature cupcake cups, or miniature Bundt pans.

orange, 1

carrots, 6 oz

canola oil, 1/2 cup

brown sugar, 1/2 cup packed

large eggs, 2

unbleached all-purpose flour, 1 cup

whole-wheat pastry flour, 1/2 cup

baking soda, 1 tsp

ground cinnamon, 1 tsp

nutmeg, 1/4 tsp freshly grated

salt, 1/4 tsp

cream cheese, 6 oz

confectioners' sugar, 1/2 cup

MAKES
12 CUPCAKES,
24 MINI
CUPCAKES,
OR 6 MINI
BUNDT CAKES

● Preheat oven to 400°F. Using the small rasps of a box grater, zest orange. Measure out 1 tsp zest (plus 2 tsp more if garnish is desired) and set aside. Squeeze orange and measure out 1 Tbsp juice. Set aside.

● Shred carrots using large holes on a box grater. You should have about 1 1/2 cups. Set aside.

● In a large bowl, beat together oil and sugar until combined, then add eggs, one at a time. Add flours, baking soda, cinnamon, nutmeg, salt, and 1 tsp orange zest and beat until combined. Fold in grated carrots.

● Line a 12-cup cupcake pan with paper liners. Spoon batter into each cup, filling half full. Bake until a toothpick inserted in the center of a cupcake comes out clean, 15–20 minutes. If using miniature cupcake cups, bake for 10–12 minutes; for miniature Bundt pans, bake for 20–25 minutes. Remove cupcakes from pan and let cool on a wire rack while making frosting.

● To make frosting: In a medium mixing bowl, beat cream cheese with a handheld mixer on low speed until smooth and creamy. Sift confectioners' sugar over cream cheese and beat until combined. Add orange juice and beat until creamy.

● Once cupcakes are cool, top each with a dollop of frosting and smooth it using a table knife or metal spatula. If desired, garnish each cupcake with a few sprinkles of orange zest.

To store Hold cupcakes in an airtight container at room temperature for up to 3 days.

key nutrients for young babies

As a parent, you have complete control over your young baby's diet. You can get him off to a great start by learning about his nutritional needs and meeting them with a wide variety of wholesome foods. Note that the foods called out below in italic type may not be appropriate for babies under the age of 1 year, especially those with allergic tendencies; consult your pediatrician about when to introduce these foods.

Nutrient	Why Baby Needs It	Best Food Sources
Protein	Protein is the building material of the body, used to construct cells, muscles, and organs. Babies need relatively more protein than adults because they grow so rapidly. A 1-year-old needs about 15 g or 2 cups of high-protein food per day.	Breast milk, formula, *other milks, egg white, fish,* cheese, yogurt, meat (especially lean beef), beans and other legumes (including *soy*), poultry, and amaranth and quinoa (treated as grains, but technically seeds); grains in combination with beans and other legumes or with cheese.
Calcium	Calcium is a mineral that helps bones and teeth grow, helps muscles function, and promotes strength. The stronger the bones grow during infancy and childhood, the healthier they will be during adulthood. Absorption of calcium is increased by the presence of vitamin C (see page 138).	Breast milk, formula, *animal milks (cow, goat)*, yogurt, cheese, *oily fish (salmon, sardines)*, blackstrap molasses, artichokes, dark green vegetables (*spinach*, broccoli), beans and other legumes (including *soy*), sesame seeds, amaranth, *fortified orange juice, soy milk*.
Zinc	Keeps the immune system strong and promotes growth.	*Wheat germ*, meats, *animal milks*, beans and other legumes, *corn*.

Nutrient	Why Baby Needs It	Best Food Sources
Iron	Iron is a mineral that makes hemoglobin, used to carry oxygen through the bloodstream to all of the body's cells. It also helps with proper brain function. Full-term babies are born with an iron supply that lasts about 6 months, and also receive it through breast milk (which contains a small amount of highly usable iron) or fortified formula. Absorption of iron is increased by the presence of vitamin C (page 138); cow's milk decreases absorption.	Breast milk; beef, lamb, pork, liver, turkey and chicken (especially dark meat), *oysters, clams, shrimp,* beans and other legumes (including soy), artichokes, potato with skin, pumpkin, sweet potatoes, figs, prunes, dried apricots and peaches, raisins, blackstrap molasses, whole-grain bread and pasta, leafy green vegetables; fortified formula and baby cereals.
Fat	As with protein, a baby's relative need for fat greatly exceeds an adult's. Brain tissue in particular is composed largely of fat, and fat helps the body use vitamins and make hormones. Mono- and poly-unsaturated fats, especially the omega-3 fatty acids, are the best kind of fats; saturated fats are not as healthy and should be consumed in moderation by adults, but are healthy for young children. Until age 2, babies should receive whole-milk products rather than reduced-fat versions.	Breast milk, formula; for unsaturated fats, *salmon,* flax oil, avocados, fruit and vegetable oils (especially olive and canola), *nut butters, peanut butter, soy, wheat germ;* for saturated fats, *animal milks,* yogurt, cheese, *eggs,* meat, poultry.

Nutrient	Why Baby Needs It	Best Food Sources
Fiber	Keeps the digestive system in good working order and regulates the amount of cholesterol in the blood. Note that too much fiber in a baby's diet may interfere with absorption of minerals and can cause diarrhea or upset stomach.	Fruits, vegetables, grains. Keeping edible skins intact on fresh produce and choosing whole grains rather than refined ones (brown rice rather than white rice, for example) adds even more fiber to the diet.
Vitamin A	Promotes healthy eyes, skin, and teeth; boosts immune system.	Liver, carrots, sweet potatoes, pumpkin, apricots, *leafy green vegetables, mango, cantaloupe, tuna.*
Vitamin C	Builds connective tissue for stable muscles and bones; increases iron absorption; has antioxidant properties, boosting the immune system and promoting healing of wounds.	*Guava, papaya, cantaloupe, kiwifruit, strawberries, orange juice, chili peppers,* sweet yellow peppers, broccoli.
Vitamin D	Promotes strong bones. Because of their rapid bone growth, babies under the age of 2 need a higher daily allowance of vitamin D than adults.	Best source is exposure to sunlight in warm climates (20 minutes, 2 or 3 times per week). However, since sunscreen is recommended for babies, but blocks vitamin D production, many pediatricians now prescribe vitamin D drops for babies. Food sources include breast milk, *fish,* yogurt, cheese, *eggs,* liver, fortified formula and foods (such as *milk*), and vitamin supplements.

Nutrient	Why Baby Needs It	Best Food Sources
Other Vitamins	In humans, 13 vitamins are required to maintain good health. In addition to those listed previously, your baby needs thiamin (vitamin B_1), riboflavin (vitamin B_2), niacin (vitamin B_3), pantothenic acid (vitamin B_5), vitamin B_6 (pyridoxine), biotin (vitamin B_7), folic acid (vitamin B_9), vitamin B_{12} (cobalamin), vitamin E, and vitamin K.	Offer a wide variety of foods to ensure that your baby gets all the necessary vitamins, minerals, and trace elements. Breast milk contains all the essential nutrients a baby needs, as does commercial formula, provided baby is drinking the recommended amount. Ask your pediatrician's advice on offering a multivitamin.
Other Minerals	In addition to the minerals listed previously, these ones are required for good health: magnesium, phosphorus, potassium, copper, and sodium.	See above.
Trace Elements	Trace amounts of these elements are required for good health: iodine, manganese, selenium, chromium, cobalt, fluoride, and molybdenum.	See above.

A note on vegetarian diets To feed a baby a vegetarian diet, work in partnership with your pediatrician. Care must be taken to feed a vegetarian infant sufficient protein, fat, calcium, iron, zinc, and vitamins B_{12} and D. Feeding a vegan diet to a baby is not recommended by the American Academy of Pediatrics.

index

FIRESIDE
A Division of Simon & Schuster, Inc.
1230 Avenue of the Americas
New York, NY 10020

WELDON OWEN INC.

Chief Executive Officer, Weldon Owen Group John Owen
President and Chief Executive Officer, Weldon Owen Inc. Terry Newell
Vice President, International Sales Stuart Laurence
Vice President, Sales & New Business Development Amy Kaneko
Vice President & Creative Director Gaye Allen
Vice President & Publisher Hannah Rahill
Director of Finance Mark Perrigo
Executive Editor Sarah Putman Clegg
Senior Designer Kara Church
Designer Ashley Martinez
Production Director Chris Hemesath
Production Manager Michelle Duggan
Color Manager Teri Bell
Photo Coordinator Meghan Hildebrand

ACKNOWLEDGMENTS

Photographers Tucker + Hossler
Food Stylist Kevin Crafts
Prop Stylist Daniele Maxwell
Assistant Food Stylist Alexa Hyman
Illustrator Britt Staebler
Copy Editor Lesli J. N. Sommerdorf
Consulting Editor Sharon Silva
Proofreaders Sharron Wood, Carrie Bradley
Indexer Ken DellaPenta

For information about special discounts for bulk purchases,
please contact Simon & Schuster Special Sales at
1-800-456-6798 or business@simonandschuster.com.

Manufactured in China
10 9 8 7 6 5 4 3 2 1

ISBN-13: 978-1-4165-9919-7
ISBN-10:   1-4165-9919-3